I0117978

AN URGENT CALL
TO THE CARIBBEAN

THE CASE FOR CARIBBEAN
DE-COLONISATION, INTEGRATION
AND POLITICAL UNIFICATION

DAVID COMISSIONG

ccp

Copyright © 2012 David Comissiong.

All rights reserved.

David Comissiong asserts his moral right to be identified as the author of this work.

This publication may not be reproduced, in whole or in part, by any means including photocopying or any information storage or retrieval system, without the specific and prior written permission of the author.

This book is sold subject to the condition that it shall not, by way of trade or otherwise, be re-sold, hired out, or otherwise circulated without the author's prior consent in any form of binding or cover other than that in which it is published and without a similar condition including this condition being imposed on the subsequent purchaser.

February, 2014.

Caribbean Chapters Publishing
P.O. Box 8050, Oistins, Christ Church, Barbados
www.caribbeanchapters.com

ISBN (paperback): 978-976-95522-9-6

This book is dedicated to the memory of those outstanding Caribbean brothers and comrades with whom I had the privilege of sharing in the struggle for our people's true liberation and from whose wise counsel I have benefitted:

Wynter Crawford, Leroy Harewood, Martin Cadogan, Rosie Douglas, Tim Hector, Ricky Parris, Kwame Ture, Kes Zacharias, Rameses Caddle, George Odlum and Ikael Tafari.

Table of Contents

INTRODUCTION

WAY back in the month of January 2009—when it had become clear that the world was beset by an economic recession that would have significant negative implications for the small nations of the Caribbean—I penned a letter to all of the Caribbean's Prime Ministers and leaders of political parties, and urged them to come together in a Pan-Caribbean "political convocation" for the purpose of designing a collective political and economic response to the massive economic crisis that was bearing down on our region.

I went to great pains to explain to them that the then burgeoning international crisis was likely to be equal in dimensions to the Great Depression of the 1930s, and to pose very serious existential challenges to our Caribbean people and nations. And I specifically drew to their attention that the inherently vulnerable tourism and off-shore business-based economies of our region had already begun to be affected, and that if we did not respond collectively and pro-actively, that we could well experience years of mass employment, collapsing social infrastructure and programmes, massive balance of payments crises, a high incidence of mortgage foreclosures, and spiraling crime rates!

But perhaps the most important point that I sought

to make to these Caribbean Community (CARICOM) political leaders was that the best and most appropriate response to the crisis would be to launch a renewed effort to collectively organise our separate small nations under the banner of a 'Caribbean Civilisation', and to establish a 'fast track' towards a political union of our CARICOM nations.

The way I put it to them was as follows:

> "We face a moment of great peril, but it is a moment that we can use in a creative and positive way. For many years now Caribbean political theorists have been arguing that nation-states such as ours in the Caribbean only make the transition to a political union if they are driven in that direction by a mortal threat or crisis. Well, like it or not, we in the Caribbean now face such a mortal threat, and we are therefore in a position to use this moment of crisis to undertake major steps in the deepening of our integration movement."

Furthermore, I spelt out in some detail the "menu" of developmental options that a collective, integration-based approach to the crisis would make available to us—a "stimulus" package based on the collective investment in new industries and structures of production; a new thrust in import substitution; new Caribbean-wide initiatives to develop critical educational, health and other social infrastructure; a Caribbean food and housing programme based on the use of indigenous resources; new collective initiatives in research, product development and marketing; and the crafting of new relations with other regions of the world.

Sadly, I received no response whatsoever from the members of our regional political leadership class. Undeterred, I sent these leaders a second follow-up letter in September 2009, and on that occasion I received two non-committal letters of acknowledgment from two political parties of Barbados and St. Vincent.

The rest, as they say, is history! In the years since my two missives, our Caribbean nations have sunk deeper and deeper into crisis, with several of them ending up cap-in-hand at the door of the International Monetary Fund (IMF), and several of them instituting mass lay-offs of public servants and truncating critical social welfare programmes and benefits.

Surely, by now, it should have become absolutely clear to us all that the only sensible way forward for us in the Caribbean is a collective march forward within the formation of a regional nation-state.

This, I must declare, is not a new notion for me. This is a conviction that I have had for many years now, and that I have tried to express through my involvement with the five "Assemblies of Caribbean People" (Trinidad 1994, Dominican Republic 2001, Haiti 2003, Cuba 2008, Barbados 2010), and my work with the Clement Payne Movement of Barbados and the Pan-Caribbean Congress. One could say that I was born and bred with this conviction, inasmuch that I was born in the island of St. Vincent to a Methodist Minister—Rev. Vivian Comissiong—who lived and worked in eight different Caribbean territories, and since I myself was educated and socialised in St. Vincent,

Trinidad and Barbados.

No—it has always been clear to me that the people of the Caribbean region are one people. There is so much more that unites us than that separates or divides us! It is therefore high time for us to come together and claim our rightful destiny as a culturally strong, secure, prosperous and progressive multi-territory nation and civilisation that occupies a place of respect in the highest international councils.

And we must claim this destiny for ALL Caribbean people; not only for those of us who currently reside in nations that enjoy a status of formal political Independence. We must regard the continued existence of European and North American colonies in our region as anathema, and do what is necessary to help our still colonised brothers and sisters to extricate themselves from the tentacles of colonial dependency, and to join us on the road to collective nationhood and sovereignty.

Furthermore, as I urged our Caribbean leaders back in 2009, we must have the intelligence and foresight to discern that we have to extend our international relationships far beyond the traditional limits imposed upon us by our former colonial masters and "establish new relations with other parts of the world." And the region that I principally have in mind is the continent of Africa—the ancestral continent of the majority of the people of the CARICOM region.

Ever since its inauguration in 2002, the new African Union (AU)—the CARICOM of Africa—has been reaching out to the predominantly black people and nations of the Caribbean, and has been inviting us to develop a deep and meaningful relationship with the nations and people of the continent of Africa.

This is an invitation that I readily accepted, and in the year 2004, my organisation—the Clement Payne Movement—joined forces with the Emancipation Support Committee of Trinidad and Tobago and with the Citizens and Diaspora Directorate (CIDO) of the AU, to establish the Caribbean Pan-African Network (CPAN) as a Caribbean civil-society vehicle for crafting such a new relationship with Africa.

And so, dear reader, it is against this background that this book is offered to you. It is my modest contribution to the emerging collective effort to push forward the inter-linked Caribbean-based campaigns of de-colonisation, Reparations, integration, political union and Pan-Africanism.

Each of these campaigns has a specificity and a value in its own right. But there can be no doubt that they all form part of a critical and crucial whole—a whole destination, a whole solution that we desperately need in the Caribbean!

This, then, is my 'Urgent Call To The Caribbean.'

PROMISE & DILEMMA
OF THE CARIBBEAN

Chapter 1

EGYPT TODAY! THE CARIBBEAN TOMORROW?

THE crisis in Egypt that caused millions of Egyptians, led by the educated youth, to engage in weeks of mass demonstrations, was 'made' in the United States of America and Europe, and, if we are not proactive in our thinking and actions, is coming to us right here in Barbados and the Caribbean.

The best way to conceptualise and make sense of the situation in Egypt is to refer back to the labour rebellion that rocked the English-speaking Caribbean in the 1930s. In 1930s Barbados, for example, the masses of people found themselves contending with an oppressive, autocratic planter/merchant oligarchy that was reinforced and propped up by the power of imperialist Great Britain. And the critical spark was applied to this tinder box of social conditions when the international capitalist system plunged into a profound depression which inflicted the additional penalties of unemployment, scarcity, hunger and hopelessness on the already suffering people.

The result was an explosion of pent up revolutionary anger and energy that left scores of people dead and injured, and that shook the very foundation of the quasi-feudal colonial order, not only in Barbados, but throughout the region.

Well, the Egyptian people were facing an almost identical scenario. For thirty long years they had suffered under the oppressive, autocratic rule of an oligarchy led by Hosni Mubarak and propped up and financed by the imperialistic USA with billions of dollars in so-called 'aid'.

But this alone does not explain the hundreds of thousands who were out on the streets of Cairo and Alexandria. The other critical contributing factor was the fundamental breakdown in the system of international capitalism that has manifested itself since the year 2007.

This breakdown was the work of the 'vampires' of finance capitalism in the USA and Western Europe who had engaged in such an excessive, prolonged and parasitical plundering of the resources of the world that by the year 2007 it had become undeniably clear that they had caused fundamental damage to the world economic system, manifested in financial chaos, industrial disintegration, excessive inflation, economic stagnation and plummeting living standards.

Compelling evidence of their greed and parasitism is reflected in the fact that they created a quantity of largely fictitious financial derivatives that is equivalent to ten times the 'Gross Domestic Product' of all the countries of the world combined. And, particularly since 2007, they have been forcing national governments to save and bail out these fraudulent financial instruments at the expense of the welfare of their own people.

Egypt had not been spared the ravages of this

international capitalist crisis, and the Egyptian people had been rocked by steeply rising levels of youth unemployment and a hyper-inflationary increase in food prices. The price of simple bread in Egypt had increased by 10 per cent each month, motivating the demonstrators to coin the slogan 'Bread, Freedom, Dignity.'

The young, educated Egyptians who drove these demonstrations were acting out of frustration and anxiety about their future. Clearly, they were seeing signs of a civilisational collapse all around them and were deeply concerned about their rapidly diminishing future prospects. It was therefore not simply about Mubarak; it was much deeper and wider than any one leader, no matter how powerful or autocratic he was!

The harsh truth is that an economic and political system is dying, and if nations and leaders do not recognise this reality and take concrete steps to distance themselves from the effects of the death throes, they will be dragged down as well.

The Barbados and Caribbean governments need to wake up. If they simply continue to do what they are doing now, their young people will eventually also come to sense that their future prospects are diminishing rapidly, and they too may eventually feel impelled to take matters into their own hands—in the streets of Bridgetown and the other Caribbean capitals!

The time for us in the Caribbean to make a decisive move has come. We can no longer afford to base our societies on the carving out of little dependent U.S. and European-based tourism and offshore business niches! Rather, it is time for us to make decisive moves to construct our long envisioned self-propelling regional nation and economy.

The political leadership of the Caribbean must rise to the challenge of casting off their neo-colonial proclivities and their narrow island provincialism, and embrace the vision of a robust multi-territory Caribbean nation, economy and civilisation that is capable of providing a bright and viable future for our children and grandchildren.

Chapter 2

THE ROOTS OF OUR ECONOMIC HUMILIATION

THE people of the Caribbean are forced to live with the humiliating reality that our economic existence hinges upon a number of airplanes filled with Europeans and predominantly white North Americans periodically flying out of such cities as London and New York and heading for Bridgetown, Kingston, Castries and the other tourism-dependent cities of the Caribbean.

We are also forced to contend with the psychological trauma caused by the consciousness that we do not produce anywhere near the quantity of food and goods required to sustain our physical existence, and that were it not for shipments of food and manufactured products from the said Europe and North America, we would be thrown into a deadly existential crisis.

Why is this so? What brought about this humiliating and dangerous state of affairs? Why do we, and our so-called leaders, accept this situation? And isn't there anything that we can do to rectify this totally unacceptable economic, cultural, psychological and political condition?

Well, let us begin by delving into our history in the Caribbean to seek out the root causes of this terrible condition of economic and psychological under-development and dependency.

It was the Spanish priest, Bartolome de Las Casas, who first rang the alarm bells about this troubling state of affairs way back in the middle of the sixteenth century, and the alarm bells are still ringing almost 500 years later.

You see, the early Spanish invaders of the Caribbean had found the indigenous people of the region operating self-reliant subsistence economies based on the production of corn, potatoes, cassava, tobacco, cotton and tropical fruits. But the Spaniards quickly conquered these people, destroyed the self-reliant subsistence economy, and established new societies based on the concept of growing sugar or some other cash crop for export to Europe, and importing food from outside the region.

It was therefore Las Casas who first made the connection between the expansion and profitability of the then new sugar industry in the Caribbean, and the Spanish colonisers' lack of interest in the local production of bread and other foodstuffs. With two casks of flour imported from Spain, Las Casas lamented, at a cost of 'ten castellanos', the Spanish colonists had enough to eat for a year, and would not bother about "sowing and setting up mills" for producing bread. "If in this island," Las Casas concluded, "there is no bread... or better bread than in all parts of the world, there is no other cause than this."

This nascent attitude of dependency might have been the product of myopic expediency on the part of the early colonisers, but it did not take long before the various ruling European establishments elevated it to the level of an article of state policy to be rigidly imposed upon their

Caribbean colonies.

As the great Caribbean historian, Eric Williams, explained in his epic history of the Caribbean entitled *From Columbus to Castro*: "Monopoly was the core of the political system, economic organisation and social structure in the Europe of Columbus' day... therefore, inevitably, monopoly became the core of the... colonial system in the Caribbean..."

Put simply, the European ruling classes were determined that their Caribbean colonies were to serve the narrow interests of the Europe-based elites, and their narrow interests alone. And since the European establishments were interested in finding markets for their own European-produced food and manufactured goods, it was decreed that the Caribbean colonies were to be denuded of such productive capacities and were to serve as captive markets for European exports.

But perhaps a dubious pride of place has to go to the French, and particularly to the legendary 17th century French Minister of Finance, Jean Baptiste Colbert, for fully fleshing out this system of colonial domination, and giving it a name: 'Mercantilism' or 'Colbertism'.

There were three essential features of the colonial system devised by Colbert, and adopted by all the other European colonial powers, including Britain. First, the colony was to be used to build up the trade of the European nation that 'owned' it. Secondly, the colony was to be regarded and treated as the 'exclusive property' of its so-called mother country. And thirdly, the interests of the colony were to be subordinated to the interests of the mother or metropolitan country.

Indeed, the British colonial system placed particular emphasis on the prohibition of colonial manufactures, and as Eric Williams explained in *From Columbus to Castro*, even went so far as to discourage the growth of towns in its Caribbean colonies. Williams cites the 1714 instance of the English Customs authorities agreeing to the creation of additional ports of entry on the northern coast of Jamaica, but only on the condition that the inhabitants were not thereby encouraged to reside in the towns and set up manufacturers for their own needs. Such a step, said the British Commissioner of Customs, would "discourage British trade and would distract the inhabitants of the colony from planting and raising sugar, which was more to the benefit of England."

And so was established the Caribbean mono-cultural economy, centred around the production of one cash crop, predominantly sugar cane, not for a local, domestic market, but for the imperial market thousands of miles away in Europe. And with this went the associated lack of local food production and the foisting upon Barbadian and other Caribbean populations of tastes for food and other consumer goods that were determined, not by what was produced in Barbados or the Caribbean, but by what was produced across the Atlantic in London, Paris and the other great centres of imperial consumer production.

But if this system of economic emasculation imposed on the Caribbean colony from outside was not bad enough, we need to note that there was a concomitant system of internal economic emasculation imposed on the black or

African segment of the colonial population by the local white colonial establishment or ruling class.

Thus, for example, in 1691 the legislature of the British colony of Bermuda forbade the enslaved blacks of Bermuda from planting or cultivating tobacco, corn, potatoes or other provisions, and from raising livestock or poultry or making cloth for their own use or for profit, under penalty of a fine for the slave-owners and whipping for the slaves.

Not to be outdone, the Jamaica House of Assembly passed a law in 1711 that forbade slaves to keep "…horses, mares, mules, asses or cattle, on penalty of forfeiture of the stock, and prescribed whipping for slaves who sold meat, fish, manufactured articles, sugar and sugar cane."

And of course, in our own island of Barbados in 1688, the House of Assembly enacted a slavery code that stipulated a series of punishments for Africans who traded in goods, and followed this up with a 1703 law which forbade whites from employing enslaved persons or free blacks in selling or bartering, and a 1779 Act that prohibited "goods, wares and merchandises and other things from being carried from house to house or about the roads in this island, to be sold or bartered or disposed of... from the traffic of huckster slaves, free mulattoes and Negroes."

These then are the historical roots of our undiversified economy; our lack of industrial production; our inability to feed ourselves; our foreign derived tastes for food, clothes and every other type of consumer fashion; and within that general system of dependency, the extreme deficiency of black Barbadian and other Caribbean people in business ownership and industrial production.

Having outlined this pathological condition, we must now turn our attention to the policies and actions required to change it, and to inaugurate new industrial economies in the Caribbean.

Chapter 3

A WAY OUT OF OUR ECONOMIC HUMILIATION

"Every student of political science, every student of economics, knows that the race can only be saved through a solid industrial foundation... Take away industry from a race... and you have a group of slaves... A race that is solely dependent upon another for its economic existence sooner or later dies."

Hon. Marcus Garvey

HOW do we rid ourselves of the undiversified, mono-cultural economy that has so plagued us in the Caribbean over the past 500 years? How do we rectify our lack of industrial production, our inability to feed ourselves, and our foreign derived tastes for food, clothes and every other type of consumer fashion?

In teasing out an answer to these questions, let us begin with the Caribbean economist who has best analysed our common economic predicament—C.Y. Thomas of Guyana.

Professor Thomas examined the under-developed economies of the Caribbean and recognised that their intrinsic dependency was based on two sets of 'divergences':

divergences between patterns of resource use and patterns of demand **and** divergences between existing patterns of demand and the basic needs of the masses of Caribbean people.

Simply put, what we produce locally is not used locally; what we use locally is imported from abroad; and much of what we crave and import from abroad is not what is required to meet the basic needs of the people for food, clothing, shelter and health care. And, of course, these 'divergences' are the result of colonial penetrations that separated the productive forces of our Caribbean societies from their roots in the domestic markets of the Caribbean.

Thus, our condition of 'under-development' is constituted by the large variety of 'dependent economic formations' that have emerged from the constraints of this separation and externalisation of productive and market forces in our Caribbean economies.

Not surprisingly, therefore, Professor Thomas proposes that the correct remedy for our condition would be to put in place two sets of 'convergences' that would reverse these separations—the first 'convergence' being a re-linking of local production and local markets, and the second being a bringing of existing patterns of consumer demand more in line with the basic needs of the population.

Professor Thomas proposes a fundamental foundational economic programme that would establish a structure upon which these 'convergences' could be wrought, namely: the establishment in our Caribbean territories of a number of basic agro-industrial and manufacturing industries such as iron, steel, textiles, rubber, wood, cement, glass, paper, aluminum, plastic, leather, industrial chemicals, vegetables, dairy products and fruit. Furthermore, the full significance of these basic industries and the basic goods that they generate will not be appreciated unless one recognises that they will facilitate the production of many other commodities, including consumer commodities, for both local consumption and export to foreign markets.

So, as the Honourable Marcus Garvey suggested almost 100 years ago, we have to industrialise, or perish! But don't take it from Marcus Garvey or C.Y. Thomas alone. Our Nobel prize-winning economist, Sir Arthur Lewis, also proposed—in less forceful language—that we have to industrialise or perish.

Sir Arthur Lewis wanted the Caribbean to develop manufacturing industries, and theorised that for a society to be able to develop and sustain industry it had to be able to save and invest at least 12 per cent of its national income. But since Lewis felt that the Caribbean societies of his era were incapable of saving and investing 12 per cent of their national income, he advocated the importation of a foreign capitalist class of industrialists— a policy that came to be known as 'industrialisation by invitation'.

Undoubtedly, Lewis went badly off-track with this latter proposal. A region like the Caribbean that has had such a horrific record of colonialism and foreign domination cannot have as its fundamental developmental strategy the importation of foreign (predominantly white) capitalists. Rather, the Caribbean must have its own programme of indigenous industrial development to which it can, selectively, add elements of foreign-owned productive capacity that will complement and not detract from the indigenous Caribbean industrial structure. And I would suggest that the foreign industrialists that we might wish to attract would be companies that are engaging in high technology industrial production.

It therefore means that Caribbean people simply have to rise up to the challenge of saving and investing the percentage of national income required to develop and sustain manufacturing industries. It should be clear to all and sundry, however, that this will not be achieved without the mobilisation and education of our people as to what is being proposed and the critical role that they must play in the entire exercise.

But how do we get the active commitment and interest of ordinary Caribbean workers and citizens to such a venture? Well, this will only be possible if we can somehow find it within ourselves to muster up the courage and resolve to finally put an end to the 'old colonial system' of race and class privilege and exclusion of the black masses from participation in the ownership of major enterprises.

We would therefore need to implement national 'Employee Share-Ownership Programmes' (ESOP's) throughout our Caribbean territories, with a view to making employees part owners in the new manufacturing enterprises. This is how we would generate interest and a widespread commitment to a national industrializing project.

Another way of expressing this is to say that we would need to create industrial regimes in which management and workers share the profits (and also the hardships in lean years), and in which companies genuinely look after the well-being of their workers. If we examine, for example, the Japanese success story in constructing an industrial culture, we will note that Japanese companies routinely provide their workers with medical and dental care, housing, hostels for bachelors, housing loans, family recreational facilities, education for employees' children, long-service gifts, stock options and condolence allowances.

The other Caribbean thinker that we need to take on board in teasing out an answer to our economic dilemma is the great philosopher, C.L.R. James.

James advocated an industry-led strategy of development as well, but felt that it should be carried out, not in separate small island states, but within the context of a unified, multi-territory Caribbean federation. Way back in 1962 C.L.R. James perceived the now defunct West Indian federation as the most effective way for Caribbean people to take part in "the general reorganisation of industrial production, commercial relations and political systems which is the outstanding feature of our world."

James was right back then, and his prescription is even more right today. Thus, our agenda must be the establishment of both country-wide and region-wide industries within the context of an economically and politically unifying Caribbean community. We must therefore let the twin processes of regional industrialisation and regional integration act upon and reinforce each other.

A politically and institutionally connected and integrated Caribbean would also facilitate C.L.R. James' other recommendation—a "State Plan" that would provide the over-arching planning, coordination, mobilisation of financial resources, educational reforms, partnership with the private sector, reorientation of consumer tastes, and mobilisation of the people. James was not advocating state ownership of the industrial economy, but rather, he envisaged the state—as representative of the people and nation—being the senior and authoritative player in a partnership with private enterprises, both local and foreign-owned.

As James saw it, the state will not only have to play a galvanizing, pace-setting role, but it would also have to provide the coordination and synchronisation of the various initiatives between industry and agriculture, and between industry and the other sectors and institutions of society that feed into and support industry. Because of the nationwide scope of the institutional changes that must accompany such a process of economic transformation, only an agency such as the state possesses the appropriate authority. And if we are talking about a multi-territory federal state, then so much the better.

In conclusion, let me assert that there is no reason why the Caribbean cannot industrialise. Many formerly under-developed nations have established powerful manufacturing industries—South Korea, Taiwan, Hong Kong and Singapore, just to name a few. There is no reason why the countries of the Caribbean Community cannot do likewise.

Indeed, there are many 'instruments' that are within our grasp, and than can be leveraged by us to foster a state of industrialisation. These include our impressive stock of natural resources across our region; our proximity to a fast developing Latin America; the existence of CARICOM, Petro Caribe, ALBA, CELAC and other multi-lateral developmental initiatives; our people's educational capacity to participate in high technology manufacturing; our ethnic and historical links to resource-rich Africa; our capacity to communicate and partner with companies of the developed world; and the list goes on.

Our fate is entirely in our own hands. It is up to us to decide whether we wish to remain in servitude as a weak and dependent people, or if we intend to pull ourselves up into the ranks of those nations that produce for themselves and stand proudly on their own feet.

Chapter 4

HISTORIC MISTAKE THAT MUST BE CORRECTED

BARBADOS, like virtually every other Caribbean nation, and indeed every other black nation on the face of this earth, suffers from the major deficiency of a lack of industrial production capacity, as well as from a lack of high technology capacity in other spheres of economic activity.

And over the past five years of international recession, the pernicious effects of this deficiency have become only too obvious, as Barbados has assumed the appearance of an impotent nation, with its leaders reduced to woefully and helplessly waiting and hoping that the North Atlantic countries would come to their rescue with a resuscitation of the flow of white tourists from the USA, Britain and Canada.

The sad thing is that it did not have to be this way. Back in 1966, when Barbados embarked upon its journey of Independence, the then leaders of our country, faced with having to decide upon a major strategy of economic development, made the wrong choice of opting for a path of tourism-based development.

Barbados' approach may be contrasted with that of

Singapore, a similar small island developing nation with little or no natural resources that became independent in 1965. Faced with a similar choice, the political leader of Singapore, Prime Minister Lee Kwan Yew—a lawyer who had been a contemporary of Errol Barrow at the London School of Economics—opted for the opposite path of industrialisation.

Prime Minister Yew has acknowledged in his memoirs that, faced with the daunting problem of endemic unemployment, the newly independent Singapore did, in fact, turn to tourism for the first two years of its Independence journey, since tourism required little capital. But he quickly goes on to point out that he and his cabinet colleagues were clear that tourism could only be a temporary stop-gap measure, and that the long term survival and development of Singapore would hinge upon industrial development and the establishment of factories in Singapore.

Furthermore, the leaders of Singapore not only opted for industrialisation, but consciously set out to give their country a technological capacity that would permit it to provide indispensable functions for industrial companies engaged in the most advanced, high technology production. And, of course, once Singapore had developed that aptitude in relation to manufacturing industry, it was able to carry it over into areas of sophisticated, high priced services such as banking, shipping, medical services, education and financial services.

If we fast forward some 48 years to 2013, we can see how right Lee Kwan Yew was. Today, Singapore is one of the most successful nations in the world, with a powerful economy based on electronics, chemical engineering, mechanical engineering, machine production, biomedical services, financial services, petroleum refining, shipping and ship repairs, and with a per capita Gross Domestic Product of US $60,688.00—the third highest in the world.

I wish to stress that the leader of Singapore had been guided by the notion that the people of Singapore must be given the capacity to play a critical role in disseminating the benefits created by forms of industrial production that were based on the newest and most sophisticated advances in technology. As a result, Singapore has not only developed the capacity for the high technology of the past half-century, but has also consciously positioned itself to be in the thick of things as it anticipates futuristic high technology developments in computer technology, micro-biology, gene therapy, cloning, organ reproduction and other cutting edge areas of knowledge.

How do we in Barbados compare? Well, the sad truth is that we have been left way behind, and are still at the level of agitating ourselves over how we can better serve and please the European and North American tourists that we are able to attract to our shores to enjoy our sea, sand and sun.

The trouble with us is that we have set our sights too low, and have been satisfied with too little. Clearly, we are not a people who are bereft of intelligence and ability. Indeed, we recently received a very pleasant reminder of the outstanding intellectual potential of our people when the story of Allan Emptage, the Barbadian computer scientist who invented the Internet search engine, hit the international news headlines. It brought home to us that it was a Barbadian who gave the world the critical invention that has permitted Google, Yahoo, Altavista and all the others to establish their multi-billion dollar enterprises.

The question we should therefore be asking ourselves is: how many other potential Allan Emptages are there among the tens of thousands of students that are being educated in our Barbadian schools?

There is no reason why we cannot set out to replicate the Singapore example by taking our people to a level where they become indispensable collaborators in the world's most advanced and sophisticated systems of production.

And, if we adopted such an ambition and approach, we too need not restrict it only to the sphere of manufacturing or industrial production. Rather, we could also extend it to putting Barbados in the forefront of new, cutting edge developments in the Arts, the Humanities, in Education, and in the provision of a range of sophisticated, high priced professional services as well.

Of course, if any of this is to be accomplished, it will require a revolution in Education in Barbados. It will also require that a new way of thinking take hold at the highest levels of government. Too ambitious and idealistic you say! Well, I don't think so. I don't think that anything is beyond the capacity of the Barbadian people. And what holds true for Barbados, equally holds true for virtually all of the other talented nations of the Caribbean!

Chapter 5

CARIBBEAN
CIVILISATION DAY

THE 1st of January is not only 'New Year's Day', but it is also the anniversary of the Cuban Revolution and of the independence of Haiti, the culminating event of the Haitian Revolution.

It is extremely interesting that the two great defining revolutions of the Caribbean, the Haitian Revolution and the Cuban Revolution, should share a common anniversary date.

The significance of this startling fact has not been lost on the members of the Clement Payne Movement of Barbados, and for some time now we have been holding meetings with representatives of various Caribbean organisations to examine the concept of 'Caribbean Civilisation', and to develop a proposal to declare the 1st of January as 'Caribbean Civilisation Day'.

What a wonderful thing it would be if on the first day of each year all of the governments and people of the Caribbean came together in a massive pan-Caribbean celebration to re-dedicate themselves to extending Caribbean brotherhood and to building the Caribbean nation during the ensuing year!

Clearly, any such celebration would need to focus on

the fundamental meaning and significance of both the Haitian and Cuban Revolutions, for these epochal events would have to be considered the two most important 'historical cornerstones' on which our Caribbean nation and civilisation will stand.

Admittedly, one can point to several imperfections of both the Haitian and Cuban Revolutions. But this does not derogate from the basic point that these two historical processes constitute critical positive breakthroughs in the Caribbean people's struggle for their nation and civilisation.

The Haitian Revolution represents the highest historical pinnacle of the aspiration to self-liberation and cultural emancipation of the African and 'Black' people of the Caribbean. It also symbolises a fundamental rejection of 'White' domination and racism, and has given us such outstanding Caribbean heroes as Boukman, Toussaint L'Ouverture, Jean Jacques Dessalines, and Alexander Petion.

The Cuban Revolution, for its part, represents an uncompromising commitment to the independence and sovereignty of the Caribbean nation, and to a Caribbean national and cultural identity built on the values of social equality, solidarity and justice. It has given us such imperishable symbols of Caribbean greatness as Jose Marti, Antonio Maceo, Che Guevara and Fidel Castro.

The issue for us, therefore, as we reflect on this notion of a Caribbean Civilisation is, how do we bring all the people of the Caribbean together—all the national populations , social classes and 'races'—in a common collective project devoted to constructing a sovereign, self-generating regional production system and society based on the values of racial equality, 'Black' pride, dignity, social equality and justice?

And when we use the term 'Black', we use it in the sense that it was used by both the framers of the first Constitution of independent Haiti, and by our great modern Caribbean academic/political activist, Dr. Walter Rodney.

The first constitution of Haiti proclaimed that all Haitians, no matter what their shade of skin, were to be called 'black'! This included even those white (in skin colour) German and Polish groups in formerly colonial Haiti who had fought with the anti-slavery liberation movement and had become citizens of independent Haiti.

This was clearly an ideological use of the term 'black' to embrace all those who were prepared to repudiate the evil 'white supremacy system', and to reject its denigration and dehumanisation of African and other non-European people.

One hundred and fifty years later, Dr. Walter Rodney enunciated a similar concept of 'Black Power', and sought to use it as an instrument to mobilise and unite the large working-class African and East Indian segments of the population of Guyana.

Rodney's message was that 'Black Power' must be large enough to embrace Amerindians, East Indians, Africans, and perhaps even poor whites, who had felt the 'lash' of European imperialist exclusion and domination.

This message was so powerful that it brought together tens of thousands of formerly divided African and East

Indian Guyanese, and threatened to obliterate the system of race-based, divide and rule politics in Guyana.

The 'dangerous' Rodney was therefore assassinated for daring to build our Caribbean civilisation!

It is a pity that Guyana and Trinidad and Tobago do not possess a Walter Rodney today.

What could be a more appropriate solution to the political and racial crises in Guyana and Trinidad than for the two largely race-based parties to come together in a government of national unity, and to challenge their racial constituencies to commit to a serious process of dialogue and relationship building?

Unfortunately, the political 'leaders' of these Caribbean countries seem to be too small—intellectually and morally—to make this type of history.

And this is why the Caribbean needs to recognise and celebrate a Caribbean Civilisation Day as we set our sights on the achievements of a multi-territory Caribbean nation and civilisation!

Chapter 6

THE LESSON OF CUBA

IF we are to ever attain a sovereign multi-territory Caribbean nation and civilisation, one of the traps that we have to avoid is ensnarement in the neo-colonial web of our powerful neighbour to the north—the United States of America (USA).

For many years now, the political and economic establishments of the United States of America (USA) have been proposing that Caribbean countries enter a so-called 'Free Trade' arrangement with the USA. Indeed, throughout the 1990s and well into the present century they engaged our Caribbean governments in intense negotiations over a proposed 'Free Trade Area of the Americas' (FTAA).

Fortunately, as a result of interventions made by the late President Hugo Chavez of Venezuela and President Luis Da Silva of Brazil, this USA-orchestrated effort was temporarily scuttled.

I use the word 'fortunately' because when small vulnerable micro-states like the nations of the Caribbean get involved in a so-called 'Free Trade' arrangement with a giant nation like the USA, they tend to find themselves imprisoned in a highly exploitative relationship. And the graphic and living proof of this assertion is the Caribbean nation of Cuba.

Of all the nations of the world, Cuba is, perhaps, the one that has had the most intense experience of what it means to be 'imprisoned' within a structure of American so-called 'Free Trade'.

Make no mistake about it, when the Americans say that they are going to confer a 'free trade' arrangement on you, they are not simply talking about trade—'free' or regulated. What they are in fact proposing is to integrate your small, vulnerable, under-developed economy into the mighty United States economy in a structurally dependent and subservient manner.

This was precisely the experience of Cuba between 1891 and 1959, the year of triumph of Fidel Castro's Cuban Revolution.

It was in the year 1891 that the then 'empire hungry' United States forced Spain—the colonial master of Cuba—to sign the 'Commercial Treaty of 1891', facilitating United States 'free' trade with Cuba and Puerto Rico.

By the 1890s, the United States' evolving system of capitalism had begun producing more goods than the United States domestic market could absorb. This over-capacity had led to economic depression, and United States' business interests therefore began searching for new markets and areas for investment. And of course, their greedy gaze immediately settled upon the potentially bountiful island of Cuba.

Expressing commitment to an alleged 'Anglo Saxon superiority', and driven by a belief in social Darwinist notions of the 'survival of the fittest', American businessmen descended upon Cuba in pursuit of their supposed God-given 'Manifest Destiny' to take over and control the entire Western hemisphere.

United States firms moved into Cuba, acquiring vast tracts of land to grow and export sugar and bananas, and by 1894 US business interests were entrenched in Cuba with some United States $50 million in investments.

Indeed, profits extracted from US investment in Cuba became so attractive that the American government was not prepared to put up with the economic dislocation caused by the Cuban military struggle for independence against Spain in the late 1890s. This resulted in the United States fabricating a justification for war against Spain, with the blowing up of their naval vessel in Havana harbour; invading Cuba in 1898; and installing a United States 'puppet' government in supposedly 'independent' Cuba.

Cuba's subservient structural integration into the United States system of power was taken a step further in 1901 when the US government wrote the 'Platt Amendment' into Cuba's constitution, and gave themselves the 'right' to intervene militarily in Cuba.

By the 1930s the invasion of American capital had totally decimated the traditional Cuban landed aristocracy, stunted the industrial bourgeoisie, and impoverished the peasants and workers. Some 40 per cent of sugar production was United States owned, 23 per cent of non-sugar industry, 90 per cent of telephone and electrical services, and 50 per cent of public service railways.

Furthermore, the de facto situation was legally

entrenched with the signing of the 1934 Trade Treaty which secured United States manufacturers a privileged entry into the Cuban market. Henceforth, it was only worthwhile for a Cuban industrialist to set up a plant in his own country if he could do so under some arrangement with the large American corporations.

This 'imprisonment' of the Cuban economy led to extreme under-utilisation of Cuba's resources and blocked any real economic growth. In fact, repatriated capital siphoned off to the United States amounted to US$369 Million net disinvestment between 1952 and 1958, while the economy stagnated and 700 000 men were unemployed.

Indeed, it was this condition of colonialist dependence, poverty and exploitation that compelled Fidel Castro and his comrades to lead a people's revolution in Cuba.

This is a history that we need to carefully examine as we prepare ourselves to grapple with the USA on other proposed free trade arrangements.

Chapter 7

THERE IS NO SUCH THING AS 'AMERICAN EXCEPTIONALISM'

THERE can be no doubt that the United States of America constitutes a danger to the interests and aspirations of small nations such as our states of the Caribbean. And a major source of that danger is the self-righteous hubris that seems to have become permanently lodged in the bosom of the so-called 'power elite' of the USA.

I would like to encourage all Barbadian and Caribbean people to make it a point of duty to deliver a simple verbal message to any citizen of the United States of America (USA) that they come into contact with. And the message is as follows:

> "You are simply a human being, no different from and no greater than the other 8 billion human beings who inhabit this planet. Furthermore, the nation of which you are a citizen is no different in legal or moral status from any of the other 200 odd nations that make up the international community. As a result, your nation is subject to the 'same/ exact' rules and principles of International Law that every other nation is subject to!"

This is a message that needs to be repeatedly drummed

into the head of every American citizen, because, somewhere along the line, they have managed to delude themselves that their country—the United States of America—is the world's singular 'exceptional' country; that they are the world's singular 'exceptional' people; and that as a result, they are singularly exempted from the standard rules and norms of International Law.

This evil and pernicious doctrine is known as 'American Exceptionalism', and it has been in existence in one form or another since Alexis de Tocqueville published his famous book *Democracy In America,* in the 1830s. But it seems that, of late, the most noxious form of the doctrine has been embraced as an 'article of faith' by just about every institution and sector of society in the USA. Indeed, it has now become standard practice in US elections— including Presidential elections—for every candidate to go before the public and avow his or her profound belief in the doctrine of 'American Exceptionalism'.

How many times have you heard or seen American politicians piously referring to the USA as the 'shining City upon a hill', or as 'God's own country'—a country that is qualitatively different from and better than any other country on earth, a country that is inherently 'good'? Well, what you are hearing is an assertion of the doctrine of 'American Exceptionalism'.

Those of us Caribbean people who, from early childhood, learnt the adage that "self praise is no praise", and who approach life with some sense of modesty, would be tempted to laugh at and dismiss these crass, self-centred, pompasetting characters. But we would be making a serious mistake if we adopt the posture of merely laughing at and dismissing these self-righteous Americans.

And the reason we would be making a serious mistake is because this self-deluded nation possesses, by far, the most formidable war-making capability on earth, and the members of the American establishment have interpreted this delusional doctrine of 'American Exceptionalism' in such a manner that they arrogate to themselves the right to inflict death and destruction on nations and governments that they disapprove of.

Let us examine just one recent case in point.

Who or what gave the Government of the USA the right to set itself up as the singular prosecutor, judge, jury and executioner of the government and nation of Syria? The short and simple answer is that the US Government possessed no such right.

International Law stipulates that it is the United Nations Security Council—a body that represents the Will of the entire community of nations—that possesses the right and responsibility to determine whether a breach of the peace or an act of aggression has been carried out by any nation or regime, and whether a punitive armed response is required. Thus, if it is being alleged that the Assad governmental administration of Syria carried out an inherently illegal chemical weapons attack on the people of Syria, it is the responsibility of the UN Security Council to investigate the matter, to make a determination of innocence or guilt, and if guilt is established, to decide upon the appropriate response.

Virtually the entire World Community accepts that this

is the settled International Law position. But not the USA. No, not a country that has wedded itself to the delusional and manifestly fraudulent doctrine of 'American Exceptionalism'. President Barack Obama, Secretary of State of John Kerry, Senator Harry Reid, and virtually all the other leaders of American society are capable of casually dismissing out-of-hand the settled, positive logic and rationality of International Law by engaging in a form of delusional 'pseudo-logic' that goes something like this:

> "The USA—because of its unique history and its unique physical and natural endowments—is a special and inherently 'good' nation, whose God-given mission is to spread freedom and goodness all over the world. And since the USA is an inherently 'good' nation, it means that its actions and policies will always be based on and for 'the good'. Thus, the ordinary rules of International Law do not apply to the USA, and the USA is therefore at liberty to take unilateral action to impose its inherently 'good' policies on a backward and wicked world."

This is the kind of 'logic' that President Obama uses to justify his sending of drones half-way around the world to assassinate men and women who have never been tried and convicted in any Court of law, and to do so even if it means killing dozens of totally innocent children, women and men who simply happen to be in the locality of the assassination target when the missiles come raining down.

This is also the kind of 'logic' that Obama used to justify his much desired 'punitive' missile strike on Syria.

And mind you, this kind of 'logic' comes from a nation that has committed genocide against its native people; that enslaved Africans for almost 250 years; that inflicted segregation and lynching on black Americans for over 100 years; that is the only nation on earth to drop atomic bombs on human beings; that used chemical weapons against the Vietnamese and other Asians; and that has illegally intervened in and invaded scores of countries, among a host of other crimes.

Let me therefore conclude by once again appealing to my Barbadian and Caribbean brothers and sisters to—as part of our Caribbean civilisation construction project—collectively resolve to take up the onerous task of constantly reminding the USA that it is not an exceptional country, and that like every other country in the world, it is not exempt from the rules of International Law!

Chapter 8

THERE IS NO 'SMALL MAN'

AS far as I am concerned, the very foundation of our Caribbean nature and civilisation must be the values of social justice, equality, democratic participation, and solidarity. I therefore hate to hear Caribbean politicians, government officials, private sector bigshots and other so-called leaders of society speak about 'the small man' or about their doing of something 'for the small man'. Just who is this small man who has to have things done for him?

Clearly, the people who make such statements have an image of the millions of working class Caribbean people as relatively helpless child-like creatures who need to be shepherded along.

The late Norman Manley of Jamaica, for example, once informed a crowd of Jamaican workers who were in the process of making and leading a social revolution in 1938, that his head was wiser than theirs and that they would be well advised to follow his instructions.

Unfortunately, Manley was merely giving voice to a sentiment shared by many middle and upper-class personalities in our Caribbean societies. Even so-called labour and trade union leaders are not immune to such elitist views. I once attended a retreat of the **Democratic Labour Party** of Barbados in which one of Barbados' noted trade unionists was openly dismissive of the capacity of lower and mid-rank party members to think and make decisions. As far as he was concerned "we", the "leaders" of the party, had to make decisions for "them."

This type of attitude is in complete opposition to the socialist vision of man and society. The democratic socialism that I subscribe to holds fast to the notion that the citizen/worker possesses the ability and social insights required to participate directly and fully in the governance of his or her society.

Those who labour under a 'small man' image of our people are also out of sync with the fundamental movement and patterns of our history, for, at every critical juncture of our history, it was the working people who discerned and showed the way forward! Of course, the outstanding example of this was the workers' revolt of the 1930s.

This is an issue that we in the Caribbean need to reflect on very seriously at this stage of our development.

We have entered an era that is characterised by the menacing spectres of neo-colonialism, re-colonisation and economic stagnation, and by the resurgence of a variety of right-wing, racist, anti-democratic and anti-Third World ideas and concepts. We had therefore better understand that we are going to have to fight all of the old battles all over again if we are going to be able to maintain the social welfare benefits, the level of national development and the quality of life that we currently enjoy.

I am of the view that if we are to stand a chance of

being successful in such life and death struggles, we must develop a system of governance in our countries that allows for the full and direct participation of all of our citizens. The fundamental policy decisions in our societies must therefore be made on the basis of the widest and fullest participation possible.

We do not want or need a 'corporatist' system of governance in which the men at the top in Government, business and the unions sit down together in some private room, work out a programme for the country and then seek to impose it on the people.

This is a backward trend of governance that, unfortunately, is becoming more and more prevalent throughout the world today. Modern 'corporatism' is a type of feudalism in which the state and the economy are run by a clique of latter day private and public sector 'barons'. It is ultimately based on the fraudulent claims of the powerful that they are wiser than the rest of us.

This is a development that we have to guard against in the Caribbean. Ordinarily, one would expect the trade union movement to be the people's bulwark against a drift to corporatism. However, our major Caribbean trade unions have over the years developed as a type of 'establishment' union, with a predisposition to disciplining the workers in the interest of social and industrial peace. This, therefore, places an extra burden on our people to be ever vigilant.

The Caribbean democratic socialist accepts that every society requires discipline but, for us, the discipline of the marketplace and the discipline imposed by the top people are both equally unattractive. We believe that the self-discipline of full democratic control offers our best hope for the future.

Our Caribbean nation and civilisation must therefore be constructed on a foundation of people participatory governance!

Chapter 9

WE ARE A CARIBBEAN CIVILISATION

AT the 1986 CARICOM heads of government conference, the late Errol Barrow made a most insightful observation about the Barbadian and Caribbean people:

> "If we have sometimes failed to comprehend the essence of the regional integration movement, the truth is that thousands of ordinary Caribbean people do, in fact, live that reality every day. In Barbados, our families are no longer exclusively Barbadian by island origin. We have Barbadian children of Jamaican mothers; Barbadian children of Antiguan and St. Lucian fathers... We are a family of islands..."

Mr. Barrow knew exactly what he was talking about; after all, his own father, Bishop Reginald Barrow, had been born in St. Vincent, his uncle Dr. Charles Duncan O'Neale had Tobagonian antecedents and had lived and worked in Dominica and Trinidad, and Mr. Barrow himself had been partially educated in the Virgin Islands.

My own experience is not unlike that of Mr. Barrow. My mother is Barbadian but grew up in Guyana, my father was a Grenadian who lived and worked in eight different

Caribbean territories, and my three brothers were born in Trinidad, Guyana and St. Vincent.

The point that Mr. Barrow went on to make, after drawing attention to the inter-connected island nationalities within Caribbean families, was that all Caribbean people are part of and share in a common 'storehouse' of historical traditions, knowledge, wisdom, and artistic, social, political and economic inventions. In other words, the people who inhabit these Caribbean territories, from the Bahamas in the north to Suriname in the south, have, over the centuries, created a common and unique culture—a Caribbean civilisation.

One of my strongest impressions of Errol Barrow was that he was one of the few Caribbean leaders who were aware of the immense variety, uniqueness and value of our Caribbean civilisation. I also suspected that this awareness constituted a large part of the foundation upon which his sense of dignity and self-confidence was built.

There can be no doubt that we are indeed the possessors of a valuable civilisation which has the potential to develop into a beacon of creativity and humanism to the rest of the world. A brief overview of our Caribbean experience will suffice to substantiate the point.

The Caribbean people have been the creators of unique social inventions in the spheres of religion, politics, art, sport and economic organisation.

Our religious heritage ranges from Cuban Santeria through Trinidadian Shango, Haitian Vodun, Jamaican Pocomania and Rastafarianism, to the numerous Afro-Baptist and Afro-Protestant churches so prevalent in

Barbados.

In politics and economics, our heritage includes our role in fuelling and sustaining the Industrial Revolution of Europe, Toussaint L'Ouverture and the Haitian Revolution, Marcus Garvey and George Padmore, Black Nationalism and Pan-Africanism, the Cuban Revolution, Stokely Carmichael and Black Power. And our experiments in political structure run the gamut from Cuban socialism to Third World liberal parliamentary democracy.

In music, we have created the steel drum, the Cuban conga, calypso, reggae, spouge, salsa, meringue, cadence, zouk and numerous varieties of folk music. Our dance spawned the calenda, the National Ballet of Cuba and a variety of Jamaican, Trinidadian and French and Dutch Antillean dance traditions.

A military tradition has been marked out by Cudjoe the maroon, Antonio Maceo and Toussaint, while geniuses like Sir Garfield Sobers, Sir Vivian Richards, Teofilo Stevenson, Sammy Soso, Usain Bolt and Shelly Ann Fraser-Price have created a distinct sporting tradition and style.

Our intellectual successes include Aime Cesaire and Negritude, Jose Marti, Jean Price-Mars, Frantz Fanon, Alexandre Dumas, C.L.R. James and the school of English-speaking Caribbean writers, including George Lamming, Derek Walcott, V.S. Naipaul, Wilson Harris, Martin Carter and Edward Kamau Brathwaite. And over the last 50 years, a contemporary intellectual tradition rooted in the realities of Caribbean life and centred around the University of the West Indies has developed. A substantial body of development-based intellectual work has been created, utilizing all of the tools of modern scientific analysis, including the Marxist system of theorizing.

These latter day intellects include economists like Clive Thomas, Arthur Lewis, Norman Girvan and George Beckford; historians like Elsa Goveia, Walter Rodney, Douglas Hall, Hilary Beckles and Gordon Lewis; and political scientists such as Carl Stone and Lloyd Best.

Surely the task of any serious leader, politician or political party in the Caribbean today must be to bring home to our people their stake in our Caribbean civilisation, and to utilise the enormous store of Caribbean collective wisdom and intellectual work to enlighten the path that lies ahead of us as a people.

We are one region, and if we are to have an acceptable future as an independent, progressive people with an identity of our own, then we must begin to think and act as a Caribbean family, making full use of our native intellect, ingenuity and natural resources.

We are, after all, a Caribbean Civilisation.

CARIBBEAN
DE-COLONISATION

Chapter 10

A CARIBBEAN
DE-COLONISATION PROPOSAL

WHETHER they are called departments, non-incorporated territories or associated states, the reality is that they are all colonies, and the Caribbean region has the highest concentration of such colonies worldwide! If we are going to analyze the condition of the Caribbean colonies, it seems to me that a useful way to group and distinguish them is on the basis of size.

One group consists of the micro-colonies: Cayman Islands, Turks & Caicos Islands, British Virgin Islands, U.S. Virgin Islands, Bermuda, Anguilla, St. Martin, Bonaire, Curacao and Aruba. (The volcano-devastated small island of Montserrat constitutes a unique individual case and will not be included in this general analysis.)

The other group consists of the relatively larger colonies: Puerto Rico, Martinique, Guadeloupe and French Guiana.

A distinguishing feature of all of the colonies in both groups is that the people of these colonies enjoy relatively advanced and elevated standards of living when compared with the majority of the populations of the independent nations of the Caribbean and neighbouring Latin America.

The group of micro-colonies, perhaps because of their small size and their small populations, have been able to move from a past of great material scarcity and poverty to their current situation, on the basis of finding economic niches within the predominantly Anglo-American international capitalist economy. And this has permitted them to produce their relatively elevated and enhanced lifestyles!

The modern economies of all of these micro-colonies are based on tourism, the provision of domains and services for international or offshore businesses, and even on the provision of second homes for North Americans and Europeans: thus, a model of dependent development, in the sense that they do not produce for themselves but depend on providing services for North America and Europe. However, it must be said that with the notable exception of the Dutch islands, none of them depend on or receive financial transfers from their metropolitan governments. In other words, these micro-colonies basically finance themselves.

The group of larger colonies, on the other hand, perhaps because of their relatively large size and/or their relatively large populations, possess economies and societies that are based to a very significant extent on financial transfers from their metropolitan home governments, a support prop that is required in light of the collapse and/or the significant inadequacy of the productive sectors of these colonies.

The French departments of Martinique, Guadeloupe and French Guiana constitute a good example of this. Not only has the old sugarcane plantation based economy collapsed, but the replacement banana industry survives only thanks to heavy national subsidisation by France. As a result, the exports of these French departments cover barely 10 per cent of their imports.

And so, the relatively elevated lifestyle of these larger colonies is dependent on financial transfers from Paris. The inhabitants of these colonies constitute two per cent of the total 'French' population and represent less than one per cent of France's Gross National Product, but absorb through transfer payments three per cent of the French national budget. Furthermore, the national and local government remain—by far—the largest employer of people in these so-called departments of France.

A broadly similar picture holds true for the American colony of Puerto Rico.

So, what we see in all of these colonies is a picture of relatively enhanced and elevated life-styles, but based on an economic sub-structure of 'dependent development'. And inherent in those sub-structures of dependent development are a number of specific mortal dangers for the people of these colonies.

In the case of the group of smaller colonies, the danger consists of the creeping reality of these small island states— Cayman, Anguilla, B.V.I. etc.—being gradually taken over by Anglo-American and European individuals and companies. I am referring particularly to the alienation of scarce land resources, business enterprises, and even demographic shifts in terms of the racial make-up of the population.

A good example of this is the Cayman Islands. The population of the Caymans was approximately 10,000 in the 1960s prior to its embarking on its modern process of dependent development. By the 1990s the population had increased to 25,000, largely through an infusion of foreigners, an infusion that features a high proportion of North-Americans and Europeans.

On the other hand, in the case of the group of larger colonies, the danger consists of the fact that, with the weakened condition of their productive sectors and their great dependence on financial transfers from the metropole, these metropolitan financial transfers will be reduced or taken away—a process that is already underway in the French Antilles and Puerto Rico.

In addition to these economic and social maladies and weaknesses there is the danger (or should I say the creeping reality) that the cultural identities of all of these states are under attack and in danger of subversion.

This danger is perhaps most keenly felt in Puerto Rico, with the American threat to the use of the Spanish language and to the traditional Hispanic-based culture of Puerto Rico, needless to say the French Antilles also face a similar threat to their Creole language and culture, while the small English-speaking Caribbean colonies find their unique communal cultures and traditional value systems under threat from various varieties of foreign cultural penetration.

All of these colonies therefore face the very real danger of losing their cultural identity!

But there is yet another danger that I would like to identify in relation to these colonies. And that is the danger that the colonies themselves constitute in relation to their brothers and sisters who exist in the formally independent states of the Caribbean and Latin America!

As we are all aware, the independent Caribbean nations, with the notable exception of Cuba, all possess very fragile and incomplete structures of independence and sovereignty. In fact we may coin a term and refer to this variety of independence as 'Dependent Independence', otherwise known as neo-colonialism. And it is therefore clear that our formally independent Caribbean nations still have some distance to go to achieve genuine independence, sovereignty, dignity, strength, self-sufficiency and psychological emancipation.

Thus, to have in our Caribbean space, colonies that constitute beach-heads of North American and European imperialism represents, by their very existence, a threat to the future progress of the independent nations.

But don't take it from me. Listen to the voice of Sir John Swan, the black premier of Bermuda who famously declared in 1982: "With the Americans to feed us and the British to defend us, who needs Independence?" Surely the last thing that the psychologically fragile independent nations of the Caribbean need is champions of such a sentiment in their midst.

Listen also to French President Jacques Chirac, who, in his 1996 official address to mark the 50th anniversary of the departmentalisation of the French Antilles, referred to the French colonies as "bridgeheads" of Francophone culture that provide France with a presence in the four corners of the world, and that, in Chirac's words, "must be ardent to defend and promote the cultural patrimony of France". Chirac also called the overseas departments "messengers" of French humanism in their respective regional organisations, such as the Association of Caribbean States.

And in this current era all of these dangers are intensified by the fact that the international Capitalist economy is in the throes of a profound recession. Indeed, the likely consequences of this recession for the dependent colonies and the dependent independent (or neo-colonial) nations of the Caribbean are as follows:

(1) The group of larger colonies are likely to experience a falling off in the level of financial transfers from the metropolitan capital, thereby affecting social services, employment levels and general living standards in these colonies.

(2) The group of micro-colonies will feel the impact of a decline in the Anglo-American/European tourist market, as well as the consequences produced by failing international businesses and the tighter regulations that are being put in place in relation to such offshore businesses by their metropolitan home countries.

(3) The independent neo-colonies likewise, enmeshed in the same type of non-productive dependent structures as the micro-colonies, face and are currently undergoing similar declines in their economic performance, employment levels and living standards.

So how do we go forward from here in the Caribbean? As we are all aware, we are faced with a scenario in which the inhabitants of the colonies of the Caribbean have consistently rejected de-colonisation on the basis of their fear that Independence will bring with it a diminution in the level of their material living standards. How do we convince the sizeable majority of people in the colonies, who have thus far rejected decolonisation and independence, to opt for a future of independence? How do we convince them that their economic security and their cultural integrity will actually be more assured under a regime of independence?

And likewise, how do we convince the people of the neo-colonial independent nations of the Caribbean to abandon their existing structures of dependent development and to reach for a future of genuine independence and sovereignty?

Seen in this perspective, it is not two struggles—one involving the colonies and one involving the formally independent nations—but one struggle involving all of us in the Caribbean!

The solution therefore can only be for all of us in the Caribbean to aim for the creation of a collective, culturally distinct Caribbean nation and civilisation that is based predominantly on an economic structure of physical production.

To this end, I would like to propose the following work and advocacy plan that all of us could pursue simultaneously right across the Caribbean:

(1) We must all advocate for the construction of a planned regional productive economy based on regional industries, and guided by the principle of delivering an acceptable minimum standard of living to all of the people of the Caribbean region.

Only the organisation of a real Caribbean Economic and Industrial Community can provide both the colonies and the neo-colonies with the investment capital, the organisational skill, and the political strength to offset the weakness inherent in the fragile tourist and international business industries; to defend themselves against the danger of having to sell themselves and their birthrights to the alien Euro-American interloper; and to consistently deliver material lifestyles to the broad masses of Caribbean people that are on par with what currently obtains in the most socially advanced colonies and independent nations of the Caribbean.

Concomitant with this, we must all advocate for the construction of the core of a multi-territory federal nation-state of the Caribbean. Once this is accomplished, we would have established a strong independent political and economic structure in the Caribbean that the currently existing colonies can attach themselves to upon freeing themselves from their colonial masters.

The best prospect for achieving this plank of our Plan of Action, I believe, is to focus on the existing 15 nation Caribbean Community (CARICOM), and to advocate for a re-thinking and re-conceptualising of CARICOM in light of these new objectives. We must set out to transform CARICOM from an economic community of separate nations into a politically unified multi-territory Federal state. Then we will have a strong core independent nation and economy to which the existing colonies can attach themselves upon the attainment of Independence.

(2) We must all engage in an advocacy campaign for the payment of Reparations by our colonial oppressors for the damage inflicted on us— colonies and neo-colonies—during the centuries of slavery and colonialism. Such Reparations should be conceptualised and presented to our people in both the colonies and neo-colonies as critical financial resources that will facilitate our move to genuine independence—critical financial resources that we will use to underwrite the construction of regional industries and crucial social development programmes.

(3) We must all subscribe to and hold up before our people in both the colonies and neo-colonies the vision of a Caribbean Civilisation based on the following three planks:

- A recognition of our shared past and of the common historical processes that have produced all of us in the Caribbean;
- A sense of our collective cultural identity as sons and daughters of the Caribbean;
- A concept of civilisational development as being much more than mere material advancement or the accumulation of material goods, and going beyond such narrow parameters and extending to the concept of development as autonomous or self-driven movement, inclusive of the autonomous confronting and overcoming of obstacles within our own civilisational space, by ourselves, for ourselves, and in our own unique manner.

(4) We must all engage in a class based political movement that identifies, targets and combats the economic and political elites (both in the colonies and neo-colonies and in the metropoles) that benefit from and therefore maintain the mechanisms of colonialism and neo-colonialism. In other words, if we hope to achieve genuine independence and sovereignty, we must be prepared to fight for it!

And within this context, we must pay particular attention to identifying and combating the United States of America's geo-political interest in keeping the Caribbean region in a state of colonialism, neo-colonialism, weakness and dependency.

(5) We must utilise the strong hemisphere-wide mechanism of the 'Bolivarian Alliance for Latin America and the Caribbean' (ALBA) as a supportive, nurturing and protective solidarity structure within which we can locate both this campaign of activism and the construction of mutually beneficial developmental initiatives. In other words, let us partner and collaborate with Venezuela, Cuba, Nicaragua, Bolivia, and all the other progressive nations of Latin America in our effort to secure a totally de-colonised, politically and economically unified Caribbean nation and civilisation.

CARIBBEAN REPARATIONS

Chapter 11

THE SLAVES WHO
ABOLISHED SLAVERY

AS intimated before, the quest for Reparations constitutes a critical plank in the strategy to decolonise and unify the Caribbean. But before we deal frontally with the issue of Reparations and its link to Caribbean integration, let us glance at the issue of the abolition of slavery in the Caribbean. Who or what was ultimately responsible for the abolition, in 1834, of the British system of 'racialised' chattel slavery?

The great Caribbean historian, Dr. Eric Williams, identified five sets of factors that ultimately brought down the system that, over 300 years, had been responsible for the enslavement and murders of tens of millions of Africans.

First of all, he pinpointed economic factors. Put simply, the 'triangular trade' and the slave-run West Indian colonies had lost their former importance to the British economy and had therefore become expendable.

Dr. Williams also cited political factors in his epic study, *From Columbus to Castro*. He was of the view that the abolition of the Caribbean slave system was part and parcel of the general, and eventually successful, struggle of the rising industrial bourgeoisie against the landed aristocracy in Britain.

Williams also gave some limited credit to both the humanitarian agitation engaged in by such European abolitionists as Clarkson, Wilberforce and Buxton in England, and Victor Schoelcher in France, and to complex considerations of intra-European colonial rivalry which motivated and drove the policy of the British Government.

But it is the fifth factor identified by Williams that I wish to focus on in this essay—the hundreds of thousands of enslaved Africans of the British West Indies and their record of persistent and unstoppable rebellion.

The American historian, Michael Craton, author of the book entitled *Testing The Chains*, has identified no less than 75 slave plots and rebellions in the British West Indies in the 200 year span between 1638, the beginning phase of British slavery in the West Indies, and 1838, the year in which the slavery system finally collapsed in the British colonies.

The record in our own little colony of Barbados is as follows:

> **1649**: a servile revolt involving slaves as well as white indentured servants

> **1675**: a 'Coromantee' plot led by enslaved Africans known as Tony and Cuffee, and betrayed by a 'house negress' called Anna Fortuna

> **1683**: a plot involving mainly Africa born slaves

> **1686**: another major plot involving hundreds of mainly Africa born slaves

1692: an Afro-creole plot led by Barbados born enslaved Africans known as Ben, Sambo, Hammon and Sampson—all elite artisans—and once again betrayed by a slave informant.

1701: another major Afro-creole plot involving hundreds of conspirators

1816: the so-called **Bussa Rebellion** which was centered in St. Philip parish but which engulfed half the island and produced such heroes as Nanny Gregg, Jacky, Cain Davis, Joseph Pitt Washington Franklin, and of course General Bussa.

These and other rebellions produced outstanding and legendary examples of courage and determination. There was, for example, the case of one of the leaders of the 1675 Barbados plot, who, on the verge of being executed by burning, not only refused to reveal the names of his fellow conspirators, but defiantly shouted at his oppressors: "If you roast me today, you cannot roast me tomorrow!" and urged his executioner to proceed.

The Bussa Rebellion of 1816, the first of the 'great' 19th century slave rebellions in the British West Indies, sent such a forceful message of uncompromising hostility to slavery that in 1819, a full three years after the Rebellion, the Governor of Barbados, Lord Combermere, was still writing to the English Colonial Office warning them that "the public mind (in 'white' Barbados) is ever tremblingly alive to the dangers of insurrection."

This oppressive and formidable fear of a climactic Black rebellion was not unique to Barbados. Dr. Eric Williams explained in *From Columbus To Castro* that "a Negro revolt in the British West Indies in the early 19th century, designed to abolish slavery from below, was widely apprehended, both in the West Indies and in Britain… In the British West Indies, it was no longer a question of slave rebellions if, but slave rebellions unless emancipation was decreed."

This assessment of the situation was borne out by Daniel O'Connell, the Irish leader in the British House of Commons who, in 1832, declared in Parliament that "the planter was sitting… over a powder magazine, from which he would not go away, and he was hourly afraid that the slave would apply a torch to it."

It is not surprising therefore that when Earl Stanley, the Secretary of State for the colonies, came to introduce the *Emancipation Act* in the British Parliament, he expressed the view that "they were compelled to act; for they felt that take what course they might, it could not be attended with greater evil than any attempt to uphold the existing state of things."

Thus, it was really the enslaved Africans themselves who, in the final analysis, were ultimately responsible for the abolition of slavery.

The critical factor was their relentless and implacable resistance!

And so it is right and fitting that we record and honour the tremendous contributions made to the cause of freedom by these heroic revolutionary fighters against slavery. Constraint of space does not permit us to note all 75 rebellions and plots; but a short list of some of the most outstanding examples is as follows:

1638: a Christmas-time rebellion on the island of Providence, involving hundreds of slaves

1690: a slave uprising in St. Kitts to coincide with a French invasion of the island

1730: the first Maroon War in Jamaica, involving Cudjoe, Nanny, and many other leaders

1735: island-wide Afro-creole plot in Antigua, led by Tacky and Tomboy

1760: Tacky's massive slave rebellion in Jamaica

1763: Cuffee's rebellion in Dutch Berbice (present day Guyana)

1769: Chatoyer's first Carib War in St. Vincent

1785: first Maroon War in Dominica led by Balla and Pharcell

1795: Fedon's Rebellion in Grenada

1796: the so-called "Brigands' War" in St. Lucia, involving many slaves

1823: massive rebellion in Demerara (present day Guyana) led by Quamina and many others

1831: the so-called "Baptists War" in Jamaica, led by Deacon Sam Sharpe.

In the words of the Jamaican historian and statesman, Richard Hart, these were the "slaves who abolished slavery." And we, their children and beneficiaries, must never forget their names.

Chapter 12

REPARATIONS AND CARIBBEAN INTEGRATION

SO what are the legacies of slavery, and how do they relate to the issue of Reparations that is agitating so many minds across the Caribbean today?

Well, in addition to the genocide that is so much a part of the story of slavery, there are also the social, cultural and economic consequences or legacies of Plantation Slavery that are still very much with us even today.

If we look at the Caribbean, all of us live on densely populated islands—over-populated island economies. We are the product of a process in which small Caribbean islands were deliberately populated with large numbers of transplanted Africans to serve the labour needs of the white colonial ruling class and their metropolitan partners.

Millions of African people were physically and culturally removed from their ancestral homelands and deposited on small Caribbean islands, and today we are grappling with the resulting problem of how to manage small over-populated island nations with meagre natural resource bases.

Another legacy of Plantation Slavery in the Caribbean is the many cultural and social deformities engendered by centuries of life on the slave plantation. I refer to such legacies as weak family structures and the entrenched culture of single-parent families. We are still grappling with that up to today—the phenomenon of 'My Mother Who Fathered Me'. In addition, there are a number of unique psychological challenges that the African population of the so-called 'New World' are forced to contend with as a result of the processes of linguistic, religious and cultural stripping that they were subjected to.

There are also the many stress-related chronic non-communicable diseases, including diabetes and hypertension, that disfigure the lives of Caribbean and other New World Blacks more than any other population group in the world, and that can be traced right back to the centuries of compressed stressful experiences inflicted on our ancestors during the slavery era.

Furthermore, there is the daunting problem of the mono-cultural economy—it used to be sugar, now it's tourism—a direct legacy of the one-crop sugar-exporting economy established by the West Indian sugar barons and the metropolitan industrial bourgeoisie, that was designed to serve their own narrow interests.

Yet another legacy is the capital and infrastructural deficiency caused by centuries of unpaid labour and the siphoning off of locally produced wealth. Indeed, one of the reasons our Caribbean nations still have to run to the World Bank and the IMF or to beg for loans from European and North American banks is that we have a deficiency of capital in these islands, because the wealth that was produced here over hundreds of years was siphoned off.

You will find it in London and other parts of Europe.

So when we talk about 'Reparations' we are talking about that too!

It would also be useful for us to recall that when the English government 'abolished' slavery in 1834, they paid the West Indian slave masters £20 million in compensation and the enslaved Africans absolutely nothing. In a sense, this was a distorted and perverted use of the concept of Reparations—compensation or reparation for the criminal oppressors. When today we look back at this perverted use of the concept of reparations two hundred years ago, we cannot help but wonder at the heartlessness and moral blindness of these people. How could they have compensated the slave master, but not the slave, who had been forced to give the slave master a lifetime of unpaid work?

Of all the major 19th century European abolitionists, only two of them raised their voices in favour of compensation for the former slaves. These were Victor Schoelcher of France, who declared that: "If France owes compensation for this social state which it has tolerated and is now suppressing, it owes it rather to those who have suffered from that state rather than to those who have profited thereby..." and Joaquin Maria Sanroma of Puerto Rico, who asserted as follows: "Do you wish a grand measure for the preparation of the slave for freedom... give him the compensation money which we reserve for his owner."

Needless to say both Schoelcher and Sanroma were disregarded. Rather, it was the opinion of William

Wilberforce that prevailed. It was he, after all, who was the first to suggest that the planters be compensated for their loss of property—our enslaved African ancestors.

And so, after 300 years of slavery, our foreparents went into the era of so-called 'freedom' without having received any compensation whatsoever for the long centuries of oppression, rape, plunder, forced labour, murder and genocide, whilst their oppressors were handsomely compensated for their loss of ownership of human beings.

As noted before, the British government paid £20 million to their West Indian slave masters. The French government paid 126 million francs in so-called compensation to their colonial slave owners, while compensation in the Danish Virgin Islands amounted to 5,500,000 francs, and in Puerto Rico to 35 million pesetas. The Dutch, however, outdid their European rivals, and in 1857 produced a 'compensation' proposal that envisaged a compensation of over 16 million florins, to which the emancipated slaves themselves were to contribute.

So, where do we go from here? That is the question now.

We are now well into the 21st century, and most of us in the Caribbean are all citizens of supposedly independent, self-governing nations. But the reality is that we are in bad shape in the Caribbean, and in Africa, and throughout the Diaspora.

In the Caribbean, our individual little island nations have been attempting to grapple with the consequences and legacies of 350 years of slavery, slave trade and colonialism alone, and without the benefit of Reparations.

Our countries in the Caribbean went into their

'Independence' with no attempt having first been made by the former colonial masters to repair the damage done by hundreds of years of slavery and colonialism. Our 'independent' Caribbean nations have therefore been trying to grapple with the consequences and legacies of 350 years of slavery—all the negative consequences and legacies, all the social deformities, the entrenched poverty, the consequences of the systematic siphoning off of wealth.

Furthermore, we have been trying to grapple with all of these burdens that we inherited, not within the context of a multi-state, collectively strong Federation, but as small, single, separate island nations. We came into 'Independence', and we have been trying to shoulder the enormous burdens and responsibilities of nationhood, and we have done so as separate small island nations that were hamstrung at the very commencement of the Independence journey by all of the unrepaired damage inflicted on us during centuries of slavery and colonialism.

Antigua has tried to grapple with all of this alone. Barbados has tried to grapple with it, alone. We have all tried to grapple with it, not only alone, but also without the benefit of Reparations—without the benefit of these former European colonial masters having paid any compensation for the damage that they inflicted on us.

After the experience of 30 years in Antigua, 50 years in Jamaica and Trinidad, and 45 years in Barbados, the results are deeply troubling. On the 12th of May 2011, Norman Girvan, the eminent Caribbean economist, delivered the C.L.R. James memorial lecture in Trinidad to the Oilfields Workers' Trade Union, and reflected on the condition that the Caribbean finds itself in today. I want to share Girvan's insights:

> In 2003 an IMF Study reported that CARICOM economies are among the most highly indebted in the world. In 2009 the UN's Economic Commission for Latin America and the Caribbean (ECLAC) reported that "the public debt of most of the English-speaking Caribbean countries has exceeded levels that could in any way be defined as sustainable."

Girvan also referred to the fact that as a result of the World Trade Organisation, virtually the entire banana industry of the Caribbean has been destroyed, and went on to further describe our economic condition as follows:

> "The Harmful Tax Competition Initiative of the O.E.C.D. countries—primarily Europe and the United States—has severely hurt the international financial services sector of several Caribbean jurisdictions."

> "The global financial and economic crisis: ECLAC has estimated that in 2009 the Caribbean subregion lost 10% of its GDP."

> "Since the onset of the crisis, four CARICOM countries have entered into major IMF programmes".

> "The latest news, which came yesterday (May 11), is that 10,000 public sector workers in Jamaica are to be retrenched."

> "Most CARICOM countries are energy-dependent

and have only survived the spike in energy prices in the 2000s thanks to the generosity of Venezuela through Petro Caribe. No one knows how long this will last."

"It is likely that the CARICOM region had become more food-dependent and food-insecure in the past 40 years. Food imports is one of the fastest growing items in the overall import bill and at $3.5 billion, are about three times the value of exports of agricultural products. The recent spike in the prices of food commodities in international markets, due largely to speculative purchases, has left most countries without a cushion and created severe political pressures."

"Caribbean countries are under severe threat from the devastating effects of climate change and sea level rise."

"The total potential annual cost of climate change to CARICOM countries has been estimated at about $10 billion in 2007 prices by the World Bank, which is about 11% of the region's GDP."

"Transnational crime—there has been an alarming increase in gun-related violence associated with the proliferation of criminal gangs warring over the drug trade in several regional countries. Jamaica and Trinidad and Tobago now have among the highest homicide rates in the world; both over 50 per 100,000, which are about 25 times the rate in Canada."

"Just a few days ago the Prime Minister of Antigua and Barbuda was speaking of the 'enormous security and economic challenges' to the region posed by organised crime, coming at the same time as countries are trying to cope with the effects of the global economic meltdown."

"Economic decline, debt, food and energy dependency, loss of policy autonomy, climate change, transnational crime—all together, a lethal cocktail."

That is our leading Caribbean economist, Dr. Norman Girvan.

So, if this is the result of 50 years of going it alone without the benefit of Reparations, maybe, just maybe, it is time that we seriously tried to correct those two deficiencies.

For some time now, I have been asking myself the question: "How do you make young people and the ordinary worker interested? How do you get them interested in something like Reparations? Why would they be interested in something like Reparations? What does Reparations mean to them?"

And as I reflect on this question, I cannot help but recall a conversation I had a some time ago with two young Jamaicans who had come to stay at my home in Barbados; two very talented young people. I was asking them about their future, and both of them said to me that they did not consider that they had any future in Jamaica. Their only interest was to get out of Jamaica: in the case of one, to get to the United States, while the other one wanted to get to Europe; two very talented young people, but they did not see a future for themselves in Jamaica.

So I began to speak to them about the Caribbean, the Caribbean integration movement, CARICOM, and the idea of political union of the Caribbean. But they responded and said to me that those things are meaningless to the average young person in Jamaica.

And I said: "Well, okay, but suppose Caribbean integration was not just about these Heads of Government meetings and the CARICOM Secretariat in Guyana and so forth. Suppose Caribbean integration, or the creation of a unified Caribbean nation state, meant instead that our separate small states were coming together to ensure that throughout the territory of our new collective nation the highest and best practices in every sphere of activity that we have developed in any particular part of our region are extended right across the entire collective nation. Would this be meaningful to the young Jamaican?"

Then I cited the example of Barbados and the sphere of Education. In Barbados, unlike the situation in Jamaica where the young student and his or her family has to pay for secondary schooling and tertiary education at the University of the West Indies, Barbados has developed a system of free education at the primary, secondary and tertiary level. So I put the question to these two Jamaican youth: "Suppose Caribbean integration or political union meant that we were going to look at the best practice in education—the Barbados system of free education—and that we were going to extend that best practice right across the region. Would the young person in Jamaica be interested in that?"

And they said to me: "Certainly! If Caribbean integration

meant that Jamaicans were going to move from having to pay fees for their secondary and tertiary education to a system of free education, then young Jamaicans would be interested; then, Caribbean integration would mean something to them!"

But, of course, if we are going to conceptualise a new vision of Caribbean integration and political union, centred on the idea of extending the best social, cultural and institutional practices, programmes and mechanisms right across our collective regional nation, that is going to call for additional financial and other resources. And this is where Reparations comes in and must be linked to the issue of Caribbean integration/political union! Reparations can provide the resources required to unify the Caribbean by extending the best practices, programmes and institutions right across the region.

The campaign for Reparations can also infuse new life and dynamism into the Independence movements of Martinique, Guadeloupe, French Guyana, Puerto Rico, Curacao, and indeed all of the remaining colonies of the Caribbean. Once the Independence activists make a link with the Reparations campaign and demand that Reparations payments be an integral part of the 'reparation package' that is negotiated with the European or North American colonising power, they will bring a multitude of currently sceptical brothers and sisters on board the Independence train.

Furthermore, Reparations payments and measures will play a critical role as we forge ahead in the Caribbean to develop our own sovereign, self-driven, multi-territory nation and civilisation.

So this is how we have to approach the future. We need now to be bold. We need to say that we are determined to build our civilisation, and that we are going to do so by connecting and utilizing the concept of the political union of our Caribbean region and the concept of Reparations.

DAVID COMISSIONG

THE AFRICAN CONNECTION

Chapter 13

AFRICAN CIVILISATION

THE Trinidadian calypsonian Black Stalin has warned us in his classic 'kaiso' entitled *Caribbean Unity* that: "If we don't know from were we coming, then we cyah plan where we going." So, let us take a look at the continent from which most of us in the Caribbean have sprung—the continent of Africa. How many times have we heard and witnessed jet black Barbadians, Jamaicans, Vincentians or Trinidadians declaring with passion that "I am not African!"

What is so ironic about this is that 150 years ago, the great grandparents of these same 'Caribbean people' harboured no doubts about their racial identity when they established 'back-to-Africa' movements and embraced such explicitly African organisations as the **African Methodist Episcopal Church.**

But the 'White World' has promulgated such a negative image of Africa with their Tarzan movies and CNN and BBC 'news' reporting, that many people of the African Diaspora routinely repudiate their African-ness.

This is a great tragedy, because as Malcolm X warned, "you can't love the fruit if you hate the tree!" In other words, if African Diasporans hate and repudiate Africa, they will inevitably hate and repudiate themselves, for in their heart of hearts they know that they are descendants of Africa!

So for our very own psychological health, if for nothing else, it is important that we combat the racist conspiracy to denigrate and marginalise Africa and to write Africa out of history. It is important that we take to heart the admonition of the great Caribbean poet, Martin Carter, and escape from the old 'nigger yard' of scorn and self hatred, and embrace a new psychology of self knowledge and self affirmation. It is time that we develop a proper understanding of the seminal and indispensable role that Africa and African people have played in the history of the world.

If we look at an accurate map of the world, not the conventional Eurocentric 'Mercator' projection map that illegitimately places Europe at the centre of the world and contracts the size of Africa and Asia, but the more modern 'Pieters' projection map, we will notice that the massive 12 million square mile African continent is truly the central land mass of planet Earth. Furthermore, if we do a little historical research we will discover that Africa was the birth place of humanity and the original home of human civilisation.

It is accepted wisdom in the domains of anthropology and archaeology that the basic creatures which many scientists believe gave rise to both the apes and 'man' first emerged on the African continent during the 'Oligocene' age some 30 to 40 million years ago.

Africa also first saw the emergence of man-like creatures

or hominids, variously named *Homo habilis*, *Homo erectus*, *Australopithecus africanus* and Neanderthals, some 5 to 3 million years ago.

And of course the momentous development upon which the whole of human history is based occurred in Africa 150,000 years ago with the emergence of *Homo sapiens*, 'man' as we know him today, in the Great Lakes region (Uganda, Kenya, Tanzania, Rwanda) of Africa. Thus, whether one believes in evolution or creationism, the continent of Africa is central to the birth of mankind.

Having been born in the sunny climes of Africa, the original *Homo sapiens* were equipped with 'melanin' and a dark skin pigmentation to protect against the strong and ever present sunlight and its propensity to create vitamin D in the human body. And this is why we can confidently assert that the original 'man' was the black man.

The original African man began moving out of Africa some 40,000 years ago into colder areas of the earth that came to be known as Asia and Europe, and commenced a process of bodily adaptation to new and different physical environments which eventually produced the various so-called 'races' of mankind.

But once again, it was on the original mother continent of Africa that man's fundamental cultural breakthrough came in the form of the domestication of plants and animals approximately 17,000 years ago.

Thus, it was in Africa that men first moved beyond the migrant lifestyles associated with hunting and gathering and settled into stationary villages and permanent agricultural systems.

This was an era in which Africa with its settled, agricultural based ethos was well in advance of Europe and much of the Asian steppe regions of the earth, which were still experiencing the end stages of a period of glaciation and were still characterised by nomadic patterns of human existence based on hunting, gathering and the herding of migratory flocks of animals.

It is important to emphasise the extent to which these two very different physical environments produced two very different culture systems. The American historian, William McNeil, explained this phenomenon as follows:

> "Pastoralists, like hunters, were parasites upon herbivores. They were like hunters, too, in pursuing a wandering life, moving comparatively large distances in search of grass for their animals... Above all else, shepherds and herdsmen had to protect their herds from rival carnivores, whether those rivals were animals or other men... **Warlike organisation and habits of violence... remained near the surface of such a life, whereas the earliest farming communities were remarkably peaceable and egalitarian...** The subsequent history of mankind in the Old World turned upon an interplay between the superior numbers made possible by farming and the superior politico-military organisation required by pastoralism. This balance tipped sometimes in favour of one side, sometimes in favour of the other, depending on ups and downs of social organisation and cohesion, and on developments in technology."

What is clear, however, is that it was the warm agriculture

based, Africa-centred, 'Southern Cradle' of mankind that invented and gave birth to civilisation'—a state of human society marked by a high level of intellectual, technological, cultural and social development.

The 'Southern Cradle' farming communities produced the earliest technological breakthroughs in the form of the plough, the lever, the wheel and axle, simple machines, techniques of irrigation, stone masonry and similar inventions, eventually coalescing into the world's first civilisation, the Nile Valley civilisation of Africa.

The high point of the Nile Valley culture system was the civilisation of 'Kemet' or Egypt, but Kemet was preceded by earlier Nile Valley civilised cultures such as the Kingdom of 'Ta-Seti'.

Kemet proved to be so central to the cultural development of mankind, that it behooves us to spend some time reflecting on this great African civilisation. Initially divided into two competing kingdoms, the kingdoms of lower and upper Kemet, the classical 'Phaoronic' civilisation of Kemet became firmly established around 3,200 B.C, when King Menes or Narmer unified the two kingdoms and established himself as Pharoah. Thus began the period of Man's highest cultural achievement, not only in the Nile Valley of Africa, but also in such satellite black or 'African' civilisations as 'Sumer' (present day Iraq) and 'Indus Valley' (present day India).

Our ancient Kemetic ancestors established the foundations of astronomy, mathematics, architecture, metallurgy, chemistry and medicine, and developed the principles of ethics, governance and religion to an extremely high level.

Tangible evidence of their achievement is to be found in the awe-inspiring pyramids of Giza; the almost universal acceptance of the spiritual concepts of monotheism and a universal God; the notion underpinning science that there are exact laws which order the universe; concepts of atomic structure and transmutation of elements; alphabet systems; and the concept of the territorial 'nation' state.

The classical African 'mentality' or 'personality' that took shape in the Nile Valley stressed the values of 'Ma'at'—peace, justice, harmony and goodness, over the values of war, and became centred on the worship of a universal God of transcendent moral values. Also central to classical African civilisation were concepts of 'matriarchy' and 'social collectivism' which stressed the emancipation of women and a belief in the values of social duty and solidarity, and which were centred in the institution of the extended family.

The typical citizen of Kemet possessed a deep conviction that man was made in the likeness and image of God, and was therefore imbued with a sacredness or divine potentiality. He had no conception of European notions of 'original sin and guilt', and was convinced that there was a divine element or spirit that infuses both man and matter. It was commonly accepted that there are principles of nature which have been constructed by a higher intelligence which govern the universe and human and natural life, and that man possesses a special (divine) cognitive gift that allows him to discover these preexisting principles.

Nile Valley civilisation was the high point of the black man's civilisation—a towering human achievement that blazed the trail for humankind's cultural development over several thousand years.

Eventually, however, the territorial state of Kemet was brought down by the combined effects of internal decay, barbarian invasion (Assyrians, Persians, Greeks and Romans) and negative climatic and environmental changes.

But so powerful was its influence that for many centuries afterwards its magnificent culture and spirit was still being reflected in lesser successor civilisations throughout Africa. I refer to such important civilisations of the first 1,500 years of the 'Christian Era' as Kush or Nubia, Aksum, Ghana, Mali, Songhai and Monomotapa among others.

Yes, the centuries long European orchestrated 'Maafa' or 'Holocaust' of the Trans-Atlantic slave trade, chattel slavery and colonialism, did tremendous damage to the civilisation of the entire African continent, but we must never allow them to foist in our minds the utterly false and evil notion that Africa is or was a continent of backwardness and lack of achievement. Nothing could be further from the truth!

And so, as we set about to construct our multi-territory Caribbean nation and civilisation, let us acknowledge that the Caribbean is largely an Afro-Asiatic agglomeration, with the vast majority of its population having been drawn from Africa and India, and let us do so confident in the knowledge that the roots from which we grew are roots that we can be justly proud of.

Chapter 14

THE COMING PAN-AFRICAN RENAISSANCE

AFRICA is not merely a place that we look to for a sense of identity and pride in our ancestry, it is also a very strategic continent that has a critical role to play in any collective effort to develop a multi-territory Caribbean nation and civilisation. Indeed, it is now being widely acknowledged that Africa is currently a continent on the move, led by the relatively new **African Union** (AU), the 53-member-state continent-wide organisation that has been entrusted with crafting the destiny of the African continent.

Ever since the year 2004, I have been involved in a working relationship with the African Union in my capacity as Chairman of the **Caribbean Pan-African Network (CPAN)**—a Caribbean civil society Pan-Africanist organisation that is headquartered in Trinidad and Tobago (courtesy of the **Emancipation Support Committee** of Trinidad and Tobago), and that has members in some 17 different Caribbean states.

The AU is currently in the process of crafting a fifty-year programme for the African continent, to be known as '**Agenda 2063**'. And in October 2013 they invited me, in my capacity as a representative of the Caribbean, to make a presentation to them on what I perceive to be the role of the African Diaspora (a worldwide phenomenon that includes the Caribbean) in Agenda 2063. The following is the text of my presentation:

"In considering the role of the African Diaspora in the regeneration of Africa, we must begin by recognising that the Diaspora consists of several components, each of which has the potential to make unique contributions to the attainment of the goals and objectives of the African Union (AU), and its proposed 50-year developmental programme known as 'Agenda 2063'.

There are, for example, the people of the Historical Diaspora—those of us who are the descendants of Africans who were subjected to enslavement and removed from the continent centuries ago. The people of the Historical Diaspora are found in independent nation states where they constitute a majority of the population; they are found in independent nation states where they constitute a minority of the population; and they are to be found in still existing European colonies where they constitute a majority of the population.

In the independent nation states where they constitute a majority of the population (such as a majority of the states of the Caribbean) they possess national governments imbued with the potential to contribute to the AU's agenda in a very unique manner.

We must also consider the people of the 'More Recent Diaspora', that is, Africans who were born on the continent of Africa and who voluntarily migrated out of Africa in more recent historical times, as well as the children or grandchildren of such Africans, born in various regions of the diaspora.

It should also be noted that members of the 'More Recent Diaspora' are to be found in independent nation-states where African people constitute a minority of the population (such as the USA, Canada, the European nations, and many of the nations of Latin America) and in independent nations in which African people constitute a majority of the population, such as Brazil and the nations of the Caribbean.

All of these components of the diaspora must be made relevant to the African Union, and must play a number of varying roles in the attainment of the goals and objectives of Agenda 2063!

In looking at Agenda 2063 from the perspective of the African Diaspora, the central suggestion I would make to the African Union (AU) is that the AU should, as far as possible, conceptualise Agenda 2063 as a gradually unfolding process in which the African continent, led by the A.U, will engage in a series of initiatives that are of mutual interest and benefit to **both** the continent and the diaspora, thereby establishing a modus operandi of the continent and diaspora planning together, working together, building new structures together, benefitting together and progressively integrating. And, of course, when I talk about 'the Continent and the Diaspora', I am referring to the people and institutions of the continent and diaspora.

In other words, as far as possible, conceptualise Agenda 2063 in such a way that the people of the diaspora can perceive a benefit to themselves as well as a benefit to the

Continent in the various projects and measures of the Agenda. Of course, this does not mean that we abandon the notion that our mother continent—Africa—should be our central concern, and that we should be willing to make sacrifices for the development of Mother Africa. Indeed, there may well be components of the Agenda which simply call upon members of the diaspora to give to Africa. But let that be the exception rather than the rule. As much as possible let us strive for mutual benefit.

It is clear that Agenda 2063 will be geared towards achieving an Africa that:

(1) Possesses a deep sense of self-worth and a strong sense of African identity and Pan-African consciousness.

(2) Is unified politically and is equipped with a central continental government and a central military capacity capable of defending the continent and its people against existential threats emanating from any foreign power.

(3) Is the functional core region of a world-wide Pan-African civilisation that encompasses all regions of the African Diaspora.

(4) Has taken concrete measures to heal and repair the damage inflicted on the continent and on its sons and daughters in Africa and in the Diaspora, resulting from centuries of European orchestrated slavery, slave trade, colonialism and apartheid.

I can go on and on outlining a multiplicity of aspirations, goals and objectives that are relevant to something as large and complicated as a 50 year Agenda for a continent of 12 million square miles and 54 nation states and its worldwide diaspora. But I will not do so.

What I would like to suggest, however, is that a critical component of Agenda 2063 should be the production of a concise Creed or Code that encapsulates in '10 Commandments' the fundamental principles and values of Agenda 2063, and that can serve as a guide or as directive principles for all the sons and daughters, institutions and governments of Africa and its diaspora over the next 50 years.

Those ten 'commandments' could possibly read as follows:

(1) There shall be a continental African system of governance that unites the entire continent politically and economically.

(2) Africa shall feed itself and shall be equipped with a self-sustaining industrial economy.

(3) There shall be zero tolerance for all notions of African inferiority, and for all forms of anti-black or anti-African racism or discrimination.

(4) Africa shall be recognised as one of the world's fundamental civilisations and shall enjoy a status of equality with all other major world civilisations.

(5) It is affirmed that there is a sub-stratum of cultural unity that binds all of the people of Africa together.

(6) The continent of Africa is the centre of a Pan-African civilisation comprised of the continent and its world-wide diaspora.

(7) There shall be no foreign military bases on the continent of Africa, and the continent of Africa shall establish the collective capacity to defend itself militarily.

(8) Africa shall be accorded a place of equality in all major international fora, including the United Nations Security Council.

(9) Africa for the Africans, those at home and those abroad.

(10) The sons and daughters of Africa shall proudly strive to live with an authentically African style of living that is self-sustaining and that exemplifies the best of Africa's cultural traditions.

Such a creed or code could be disseminated throughout Africa and the diaspora, and could be used as an instrument to keep us focused, unified, motivated and on track.

But, after being sufficiently motivated and focused, what are some of the concrete ways in which the diaspora can play a role or be involved in attaining the Vision of Agenda 2063? My concrete suggestions are as follows:

(1) THE REGIONAL NETWORKS

I think we have to begin with those diaspora structures and organisations that have been consciously developed for the purpose of engaging with the AU in establishing and implementing the AU's diaspora outreach initiative, otherwise known as the 'Sixth Region' project.

Pan-African activists and organisations from every region of the diaspora need to bestir themselves and act with discipline and commitment to form themselves into regional Pan-Africanist Networks that will engage with the AU in an organised manner.

These Regional Networks will need to take responsibility for identifying the legitimate regional representatives who will occupy the seats reserved for the various regions of the diaspora in the Economic Social and Cultural Council (ECOSOCC) of the African Union and in the various Cluster Committees of ECOSOCC.

The regional networks must also become the critical on-the-ground infrastructure through which the AU agenda in general, and Agenda 2063 in particular, will be disseminated to the people of the African Diaspora.

The regional networks will also have to play a critical role in helping to mobilise the human and financial resources of the diaspora communities and nations that they represent, for deployment in projects that are relevant to the development of Africa and its diaspora.

In similar vein to the Republic of India, the AU will have to develop a programme under which sons and daughters of the African Diaspora will officially be certified as 'Citizens of African Origin', and will receive certificates or other forms of documentation that will entitle them to some form of special or preferential status in all member nations of the AU. And I hasten to add, not preferential in relation to indigenous citizens of those countries, but preferential in relation to non-African foreigners.

Needless to say, the regional networks will have to play

a critical role in helping to put such a programme in place. This type of programme could be the answer to diasporans who are agitating for a right of return to the continent and the right to some form of dual citizenship.

(2) AFRICAN UNION OUTREACH PROJECTS TO THE DIASPORA

The AU must move with haste to establish mechanisms and programmes that are designed to mobilise and harness the human and financial resources of the Diaspora. I refer to such projects as the establishment of a Pan-African Mutual Fund, Pan-African Development Bond issues, and a Pan-African Volunteer Programme.

Such projects will have to be carried out in partnership with institutions of the Diaspora, and will have to be fully supported by the regional networks.

(3) ESTABLISHMENT OF DEPARTMENTS OR MINISTRIES OF PAN-AFRICAN AFFAIRS

The AU needs to facilitate the diaspora to connect with and engage with the African continent by mandating every member state of the AU to establish ministries or departments of Pan-African or Diaspora Affairs as part of the structure of government.

Independent black nation states of the diaspora must also be encouraged to establish such governmental institutions. One outstanding example of this is the Government of Barbados' Commission for Pan-African

Affairs. Caribbean Pan-Africanists must lobby their governments to follow the Barbados example and establish governmental agencies designed to facilitate engagement with Africa and other regions of the diaspora.

This type of governmental infrastructure on the continent and in the diaspora is critical for facilitating developmental partnerships, sharing of expertise, and the building of strong relationships across our Pan-African world.

(4) A PAN-AFRICAN EDUCATIONAL PROGRAMME

A concerted effort needs to be made to develop and deploy a formal and informal educational programme devoted to fostering the historical consciousness of the people of Africa and the Diaspora, and to fostering Pan-African consciousness. To this end, the AU should make an effort to partner with the nations of the Caribbean Community and with outstanding black educational institutions and educators from across the African Diaspora to conceptualise, plan and execute such a model Pan-African educational programme, inclusive of the production of relevant educational materials.

(5) ESTABLISH PAN-AFRICAN STRUCTURES IN AFRICA'S INTERNATIONAL ENGAGEMENTS

The AU should seek to establish Pan-Africanist structures and relationships within every international or multi-national organism or programme that it is involved in. For example, the countries of South America (led by Venezuela) are engaged in an on-going 'African/South American Summit' with Africa. The African nations involved in the 'African/South America Summit' should seek to build into that arrangement a Pan-Africanist structure that permits them to engage in some way with the African organisations and communities of the South American sub-continent. (A similar approach can be taken in respect of the AU's engagement with the European Union and with the countries of the Pacific region.)

In this manner, the AU will be grasping every possible opportunity to establish contact and relationships with members of Africa's Diaspora. And this will be of particular importance in relation to regions of the Diaspora in which African people constitute a minority—often an exploited minority—of the population.

(6) REPARATIONS

The sons and daughters of Africa and the African Diaspora have all had the common experience of suffering the negative consequences that have emanated from centuries of European-orchestrated slavery, slave trade and colonialism, and therefore share a collective vested interest in healing and repairing the damage and injury that we have suffered. This quest for repair and healing is known as the campaign for Reparations.

Virtually every region of the African World has evinced an interest in pursuing a campaign for the securing of

Reparations: Reparations which take the form of our own self-generated and self-made repairs on ourselves and our societies; and Reparations which take the form of compensatory payments and programmes that are extracted, as a matter of International Law, from the relevant European former colonial governments.

The OAU, for example, led the way in the early 1990s with the proclamation of the Abuja Declaration on Reparations, and the establishment of the OAU's Group of Eminent Persons on Reparations and a Reparations Commission. Furthermore, all across the African Diaspora, the black civil society has established Reparations organisations. And recently, the 15 independent member nations of the Caribbean Community (CARICOM) established a CARICOM Reparations Commission and mandated every CARICOM member state to establish national Reparations Commissions, and the University of the West Indies to establish a Reparations Research Unit.

I therefore wish to suggest that the Reparations issue and the international campaign to secure Reparations constitutes an instrument that can be used to unite Africa and the Diaspora in a common cause.

The AU should therefore join forces with CARICOM in pursuing a campaign for Reparations. Once this is done, it is clear that the joint CARICOM/AU Reparations Campaign will provide a structure around which Diaspora civil society organisations of North America, Central America, South America and Europe will be able to mobolise and make common cause.

Such an all-embracing Pan-African Reparations

Campaign will of necessity cause us to research and investigate our common history, our biological and cultural kinship, our common predicament, and common solutions to our predicament. It will also cause us to engage in collective diplomatic and legal efforts in the international arena.

In short, the pursuit of Reparations will foster Pan-African unity and development.

(7) A PAN-AFRICAN COMMONWEALTH OF NATIONS

Just as Britain has taken the initiative to establish a British Commonwealth of nations that experienced a history of British colonialism, and just as South America, in a more positive vein, has engaged with Africa in establishing the 'Africa/South America Summit', the AU should take the initiative to establish a 'Pan African Commonwealth of Nations' comprised of all of those independent nations that are totally or predominantly black or African, along with selected countries that possess sizeable African populations and that have evinced a strong desire to engage with Africa.

The countries that I have in mind are the 54 countries of Africa, the 15 countries of the Caribbean Community, and such Latin American and Caribbean countries as Cuba, Brazil, Venezuela and Nicaragua among others.

This project will provide a powerful and valuable state-centred mechanism for the building of Pan-African unity, and for achieving many of the goals of Agenda 63."

I would like to humbly suggest that the proposals that I urged upon the AU in this presentation would not only foster the mutual development of Africa and the Caribbean, but that several of them can be converted into strategies that the people and civil society organisations of the Caribbean can employ in emerging with and fostering the work of CARICOM and the CARICOM Secretariat.

DAVID COMISSIONG

CARIBBEAN
POLITICAL UNION

Chapter 15

ONWARD TO A UNION OF CARIBBEAN STATES

NOW that we have waded through all of the preliminary issues pertaining to our nascent Caribbean nation and civilisation, it is time for us to come to grips with the most immediate and pressing matter confronting us—how do we go forward from here to transform our Caribbean Community (CARICOM) into a politically unified multi-territory nation, thereby establishing the critical mechanism and infrastructure that is needed to pave the way towards a totally de-colonised and integrated multi-lingual Caribbean?

Let us begin by giving some historical context, inspiration and perspective to this issue from what many might consider a most unlikely source—namely, the United States of America! In this era of crisis, when virtually every single Caribbean country seems destined to end up in the clutches of the dreaded International Monetary Fund, it would do well for the people and nations of the Caribbean Community (CARICOM) to reflect on that phase in the history of the United States of America (USA) that has come to be known by historians as the 'Critical Period', the years between 1783 and 1789.

The year 1783 was the year in which the thirteen former British colonies of North America, having fought a 7-year war against British imperialism, finally secured their Independence with the signing of the Treaty of Paris. But the independent USA that emerged in 1783 was not the strong, successful, federal Republic that we know today. Rather, it was a loose and weak confederation of 13 sovereign states, not too different from the so-called 'community' of sovereign states that is our currently existing CARICOM.

The USA of 1783 was the creature of the 1777 Articles of Confederation, a constitutional document that merely provided for a relatively powerless unicameral congress in which each state possessed one vote, which was cast by 'delegates' appointed by the legislature of the state. The confederation had no powers of taxation; no executive President; no formal constitutionally stipulated executive departments or officers; and not even a Federal Court!

This initial loose and weak 'Confederation' of the United States of America was so ineffectual that by the year 1786 the nation faced total collapse and the prospect of reconquest by Britain. Bereft of any firm guidance by a national government, the country had become generally chaotic. Congress could, and did, pass resolutions and enact ordinances, but it had no powers to carry its decisions into effect and no courts capable of enforcing its orders either on individuals or on states. The upshot was that foreign trade came to a standstill, agriculture sank into depression, commercial debts became uncollectable, and the national government, in the form of Congress, dropped to an abysmal level of powerlessness and general disregard.

It was in this dire situation of existential crisis that a small number of outstanding statesmen and patriots emerged with a plan and with the will and commitment to transform the loose and weak Confederation into the strong and nationally integrated Federal Republic of the USA that we know today. The heroes that I refer to are James Madison, Alexander Hamilton, John Jay, Benjamin Franklin and George Washington.

Madison led the way when, in 1786, he was successful in getting the 13 states to agree to hold an 'inter-state' meeting at Annapolis in Maryland to "consider the extension of national authority to the regulation of commerce." Of course, this modest 'meeting', with its modest agenda, was merely the thin edge of the wedge that was to be used in securing a fundamental overhaul of the Constitution of the country.

The Annapolis Convention was deliberately cut short, but not before it had drawn up a proposal to congress and the 13 states that a follow-up convention be held the following year in Philadelphia for the larger purpose of making "the constitution of the Federal Government adequate to the exigencies of the Union."

The rest, as they say, is history. Not only was the Philadelphia Convention held in 1787, but it turned out to be one of the most creative convocations in history, producing a thoroughly revamped constitution that established the national government of the USA that we are all familiar with today, inclusive of the office of

President, the Senate, the House of Congress, and the Supreme Court. The new constitution also provided the basis for the creation of the departments of State, Treasury, War, and the list goes on.

Following upon the successful Philadelphia Convention of 1787, Madison, Hamilton and Jay set out on a mission to convince the 13-state government to ratify the new Constitution, and after some two years of heroic endeavour—including the publication and dissemination of the 85 essays contained in the 'Federalist Papers'—they were spectactularly successful. By 1789 all of the States had ratified the new constitution, and the new nation, after 15 years of trial and error, finally had the solid system of national governance that could provide for its integration, military protection and economic and social development.

What, you may well ask, does all of this have to do with us in CARICOM? Well, I would like to suggest that just as the visionary statesmen of the USA were not content to accept the deficient first version of their new multi-territory country and were determined to press onward until they transformed it into a structure that was capable of dealing effectively with the challenges facing their new nation, we too must have a similar vision and commitment in relation to our CARICOM.

Surely we can all see that the current governance and integration mechanism that we possess in our Caribbean Community (CARICOM) is not strong enough or comprehensive enough to deal with the very serious economic, social, and cultural challenges that are bearing down upon us. And if this is the case, why shouldn't we have a similar resolve to revisit our regional Constitution—our Treaty of Chaguaramas—and to do what is necessary to further develop and transform it, so that we can give ourselves that most precious of gifts: a regionalised 'national' governance structure that is capable of elevating our Caribbean Community to the position of strength, progress, glory and honour that is its rightful due!

It is against this background, therefore, that I propose to look at the developmental needs of our CARICOM region, and to consider how we can further develop the currently existing CARICOM institutions and structures to adequately accommodate and service these needs.

I am proceeding on the basis of my firmly held conviction that the constitution of a genuine regional nation-state can be brought forth organically out of the currently existing Treaty of Chaguaramas. Indeed, what I am proposing to do is to use the existing Treaty of Chaguaramas to produce a blueprint or plan for the construction of a regional nation-state that is tailored to fit our unique circumstances and needs in the Caribbean. And it is my hope that, just like in the United States of America, statesmen and patriots would be willing to come together to take what is envisioned and planned (or some further modified version of it), and convert it into reality.

Chapter 16

THE RATIONALE FOR A FEDERATION

IN this chapter I am going to be arguing that we Caribbean people can establish a Federation of the Caribbean; that we can do so by simply evolving and extending our already existing Treaty of Chaguaramas; and that when we do so, we don't necessarily have to relinquish the status of nationhood that our individual island nations currently possess, nor compromise the unique cultural identities of our various mini-states.

But let us begin by reminding ourselves why we need to establish a strong multi-territory nation-state in the Caribbean.

The harsh reality is that the small states of the Caribbean cannot seriously face up to the massive threats posed by a crisis-ridden and imperialist-oriented international capitalist system with a protective mechanism that is as weak and deficient as our currently existing Caribbean Community (CARICOM). We need something of much greater strength and substance! We need something that more closely approximates a multi-territory nation-state equipped with a federal or confederal government.

There is no reason why we should not set our sights on achieving something that 'approximates' a multi-territory nation-state—a Federation or Confederation of the Caribbean—in light of the fact that we share a common geographical space and a common history, kinship and cultural identity.

Furthermore, and just as importantly, we already possess the basic structure of a regional national Constitution in the form of the 'Revised Treaty of Chaguaramas'. All we need to do now is to consciously evolve and further develop the 'Revised Treaty of Chaguaramas', and commit ourselves to seriously implementing the product of such an exercise in constitutional development.

But let me hasten to add that the 'constitutional product' that we are aiming for is one that will stop short of being the type of traditional unitary or federal state that would require the wiping out of individual island statehood and sovereignty. Having the strength of a Federation or Confederation of the Caribbean does not necessarily mean that we have to dismantle the status of 'statehood' or 'nationhood' that our Caribbean mini-nations currently possess.

There is no reason why we cannot advance to a Federation or Confederation while at the same time maintaining the de jure 'nation' status of Barbados, Jamaica, St. Vincent, Trinidad and Tobago, and the other member states of CARICOM. There is no reason why these states cannot continue to possess such political institutions as a government, a state parliament and law courts! And there is also no reason why the establishment of a Federation or Confederation of the Caribbean should prevent Barbados, Jamaica, Dominica and the others from

DAVID COMISSIONG

continuing to preserve and develop their unique cultural identities!

Of course, one of the compelling reasons for wanting to maintain the 'nation' status of our CARICOM member states is centered on the power and clout in international organisations that comes with such status. At present, our CARICOM states possess 14 votes at the United Nations, at the Organisation of American States, and in several other international organisations. This is a source of strength that it would do us well to maintain.

Basically, what I am saying is that the 'Further Revised Treaty of Chaguaramas' that I am proposing must aim at a regional constitutional structure that is designed to preserve our existing strengths and to eradicate our weaknesses.

We must set about to create a Federation or Confederation in which equal state partners voluntarily associate in order to perform specific tasks collectively, and to bestow upon themselves an international persona that will deliver a certain level of regard and respect in the international arena. But we must go about creating these supra-national regional structures that are so essential to fostering the unimpeded growth of our regional economy and to securing for us other social and political benefits, without at the same time negatively impinging on the unique cultural identities of our various mini-states.

The currently existing weaknesses or needs that we must tackle through the creation of a regional multi-territory Federation or Confederation are as follows:

(1) The need to facilitate and energise economic development based on the establishment of regional industries and on the mobilisation and creative combining of the resources of the various territories.

(2) The need to end the wasteful duplication of political and administrative activity and structures in our sub-region, and to better organise and synchronise such structures.

(3) The need to give institutional and political expression to the deeply rooted sense of Caribbean nationhood felt by the people of the CARICOM territories.

(4) The need to develop a foreign policy and a collective platform for dealing with the outside world that is strong, meaningful and coherent, and that is effectively articulated.

(5) The need to deliver to the people of our CARICOM territories a common and elevated level of human and civil rights, living standards and life opportunities.

(6) The need to give to the people of our CARICOM territories a sizeable area of living space in which they would be free to roam and explore, in search of life opportunities and individual or family destinies.

(7) The need to bestow upon the people of our sub-region a collective nation-type structure that is large enough, strong enough and self-reliant enough to elicit appropriate respect and regard from the nations of the international community.

Our next step, therefore, is to consider how the Caribbean patriots and statesmen of this era can modify and further evolve the 'Revised Treaty of Chaguaramas' in order to produce a constitutionally undergirded regional institutional structure—a Federation or Confederation—that is capable of helping us to grapple with and satisfy these critical needs.

The Caribbean statesmen and patriots of the 1960s and 70s: Errol Barrow, Forbes Burnham, Eric Williams, Michael Manley, Vere Bird, took us as far as the currently existing Treaty of Chaguaramas. Let us not reject or downplay their handiwork, but rather let us see how we can further evolve and develop their (and our) Treaty of Chaguaramas, in order to give us our much needed and desired end-product—a Federation or Confederation of the Caribbean!

Chapter 17

A FURTHER REVISED
TREATY OF CHAGUARAMAS

AS we seek to go forward in the Caribbean during this period of crisis, the central question that we need to consider is: How can the 'Revised Treaty of Chaguaramas' be so organically evolved that it is made to give birth to a regional entity that approximates a multi-territory nation state equipped with a federal or confederal government? In other words, how can we utilise the Treaty of Chaguaramas to give birth to a Federation or Confederation of the Caribbean?

And of course, we must begin with the highest organs and institutions of a nation state: a national Executive, Parliament and Head of State. How can a collective, region-wide Executive, Parliament and Head of State emerge organically from the Revised Treaty of Chaguaramas?

Well, let us begin with the institution of Parliament. Let us remind ourselves that the Revised Treaty of Chaguaramas has already established a Conference of Heads of Government, and has also made provision for an Association of Caribbean Community Parliamentarians.

My proposal, therefore, is that we establish a bi-cameral 'Federal Assembly' in which the upper chamber, to be known as the 'Council of States', would be comprised of the Heads of Government of the 15 CARICOM member states. All member states would therefore have equal representation in the upper house of the Federal Assembly.

The lower house, to be known as the 'National Council', would be constructed along the lines of the Association of Caribbean Community Parliamentarians, and would therefore consist of sitting members of the Houses of Assembly of the 15 CARICOM member states, who are selected by their fellow parliamentarians to serve as members of the lower chamber of the Federal Assembly. In other words, they will serve both as parliamentarians of their national House of Assembly and as Federal parliamentarians. And of course, seats in the National Council will bear a relationship to the size of populations of the 15 CARICOM member states. Thus, the larger the population a member state has, the larger will be its allocation of seats in the lower chamber of the Federal Assembly.

Under my proposal, the Federal Assembly, comprised of the Council of States and the National Council, would convene in different state capitals of the new 'Federation', four times a year, for sittings lasting three weeks each, and would carry out the following functions:

(1) Enact Federal legislation;
(2) Consider and make constitutional amendments;
(3) Approve the members of the Federal Cabinet;
(4) Approve the Federal budget;
(5) Elect the Chancellor or Head of the Federal Civil Service;

(6) Elect the members of the federal court—the Caribbean Court of Justice;

(7) Elect the Commander-in-Chief of the Federal army;

(8) Establish Standing Parliamentary Committees that correspond to the various Ministries of the Executive, and that would provide continuity to the legislative duties of the Assembly during the periods when the Assembly is not sitting.

As indicated earlier, the parliamentarians of the 'Federation' would function in dual capacities—they would remain Parliamentarians and/or Heads of Government of their territorial states, while at the same time, devoting a sum total of three months of the year to service as legislators of the Federation. In this era of modern communications technology, this is easily doable.

The members of the Executive or Cabinet of the Federation would, however, have to be full time officers! Let us now consider the Federal Cabinet.

The federal Executive or Cabinet, to be known as the 'Federal Council', would emerge out of such **already existing** organs of CARICOM as the Council of Ministers responsible for CARICOM Affairs, the Council for Finance & Planning, the Council for Trade & Economic Development, the Council for Foreign & Community Relations, the Council for Human & Social Development, and the Legal Affairs Committee.

These various organs of CARICOM consist of the Ministers of Government of the 15 member states who are responsible for these spheres of activity. For example, the

Council for Foreign & Community Relations consists of the various Ministers of Foreign Affairs of the CARICOM member states.

Since the Federal Ministers will be full-time officers, it means that no sitting state Minister of Government can become a Federal Minister. Rather, my proposal is that at the commencement of every term of government of the Federation, the state Ministers who comprise the membership of the various Councils of CARICOM, would be brought together for the purpose of selecting an outstanding CARICOM citizen to serve as the Federal Minister of the portfolio covered by their particular Council.

A practical example may help to elucidate this point. Let us take the CARICOM Council for Trade & Economic Development. This Council brings together the territorial Ministers of Trade and Economic Affairs. Under my proposal, these Ministers will come together and identify and select an outstanding CARICOM citizen who can be entrusted with the Federal Ministry of Trade and Economic Affairs. This type of approach might, for example, permit the Federation to have a Norman Girvan—the Caribbean's outstanding development economist—as its Minister of Trade and Economic Affairs.

However, the Council's selection of a Minister-elect would not be the end of the Ministerial selection process! The next stage of the process would be for the selection to be forwarded to the Federal Assembly for approval by both chambers of the Assembly. Once this is achieved, then the Minister would be appointed and would take control of his particular federal Ministry.

Of course, the Federal Cabinet will consist of all the Ministers of the Federation—the Ministers of Trade & Economic Affairs, Foreign Affairs, Finance & Planning, Transport & Power, Human & Social Development, Justice & Police, and Defence & Security—as well as the Chancellor or Head of the Federal civil service.

The cabinet will obviously be a collegial body, and, I am proposing that, on a revolving annual or bi-annual basis, it should select one of its members to be Chairman of the Cabinet and, in effect, President of the Federation for that one or two year period. Of course, what this signifies is that to all intents and purposes the Cabinet will constitute the collegial Head of State of the Federation. Furthermore, this would also mean that no one territory will monopolise the Presidency of the Federation.

This then would be the basic outline of the government of a new Federation or Confederation, but one which, I again hasten to add, would not require the wiping out of individual island statehood or 'nationhood', nor the dismantling of the unique cultural identities of the various island and mainland states.

In the next chapter we will consider other subsidiary elements of the proposed Federal or Confederal governance structure, and go on to challenge such current political leaders of CARICOM as Prime Ministers Ralph Gonsalves, Portia Simpson-Miller, Kenny Anthony, Roosevelt Skerrit, Freundel Stuart, Denzil Douglas, Baldwin Spencer, Keith Mitchell, Perry Christie, Dean Barrow, and Kamla Persad-Bissessar to rise to the challenge of making an indelible mark on history by taking our region to the next phase of its historical journey— the establishment of a Federation or Confederation of the Caribbean.

Chapter 18

NEW FEDERAL ASSISTANCE, POWER & AUTHORITY

WE have spent the last three chapters arguing that Caribbean people can and should establish a Federation or Confederation of the 15 Caribbean Community (CARICOM) states; that we can do so by simply evolving and extending our already existing Treaty of Chaguaramas; and that when we do so we don't necessarily have to relinquish the status of 'nationhood' that our individual island nations currently possess, nor compromise the unique cultural identities of our various mini-states.

One of the fundamental things we will accomplish by welding our various mini-states together politically is the creation of a powerful new collective Federal government that will add to the effectiveness of our individual island governments, and bring to bear additional resources, focus and energy on fostering the development of our people. Thus, a political union will strengthen us rather than weaken us. A new, collective, Federal central government should therefore be viewed in terms of its ability to increase our capacity for self development.

The state of Florida in the United States of America, for example, possesses a state government that fosters the development of the territory and people of Florida. But it is also served by a federal government—the Federal Government of the United States of America—which brings additional attention and resources to bear on the development of the territory and people of Florida. Why then should we Caribbean people wish to continue to deny ourselves the additional developmental assistance of a collective 'Federal' government?

Furthermore, once we establish a collective, unified Federal government, we will be able to rationalise and scale back some of the costly bureaucracy of our individual island governments. Why, for example, should a small region like the Caribbean be financing the costs of fourteen different embassies in New York and Washington, when one would suffice? The establishment of a 'political union' of the Caribbean will permit us to rationalise operations and save precious revenue in several spheres.

Surely, it must be clear to all thinking Caribbean people that if the countries of CARICOM were to unite politically they would, overnight, equip themselves with a number of new and powerful instruments that could be deployed to generate economic development and provide enhanced life opportunities for their people.

Of course, the highest and most powerful such new instruments would be a Federal Executive equipped with well defined management and administrative responsibilities in relation to the entire territory and population of the Federation.

Clearly, the Federal Executive would have to assume responsibility for the establishment of new, collectively owned regional industries, and for overseeing the efficient functioning of a single market and economy. Furthermore, the Federal Executive could also be mandated to ensure that every geographical area of the Federation attains an agreed upon 'minimum' level of development and human welfare, since the whole purpose of having a political union would be to ensure a lifting of the quality of life for all citizens of our Federation or Union.

The existence of a political union would also provide us with a priceless opportunity to create a 'common currency', and to use the initial issuing of this new money as a mechanism for financing new developmental projects.

Let us spend a little time explaining how this would work. Firstly, let us recognise that a Federation or 'Union of Caribbean States' would have to be equipped with a collectively owned 'National Bank', and would also have to possess a common 'currency' or 'money'—a new Union of Caribbean States dollar.

And, naturally, the Federal Executive would possess the power to issue the new currency of the Union, and would do so through a newly established National Bank. Furthermore, the initial quantities of the currency could be issued through the 'National Bank' in the form of 'credit' or loans to the various island governments, state enterprises and appropriate private sector entities for the sole purpose of financing developmental projects designed to add to the productive capacity of our sub-region.

The issuing of credit for the purpose of increasing production will not have an inflationary effect, and would allow the Federation or Union of Caribbean States to gradually phase in the common currency while at the same time phasing out the various island currencies over a period of time. Thus, with careful management of the new and old currencies we can avoid the dangers of inflation and foreign exchange leakage, while at the same time boosting economic diversification and output.

One can clearly see, therefore, how the establishment of a Federal Executive, a National Bank and a common currency would provide us with a new source of capital, and with a new and enhanced capacity to finance industrial, agricultural, fisheries, manufacturing, airport construction, and a host of other developmental projects.

As the Federation or Union launches its new 'Caribbean' brand, it will also have to invest in creating relevant infrastructure and linkages running from Suriname in the south, right up the chain of islands to the Bahamas in the north—infrastructure for the construction of multi-territory regional industries. And clearly, one component of this nexus of infrastructure and linkages will have to be a system of high speed ferries and a unified national airline capable of the mass transportation of people and goods at very reasonable rates.

The Federation or Union will also require an inter-linked mass media system capable of providing it with the type of intimate and intensive news coverage that the American news networks provide for the people of the U.S.A. Not only will this help to solidify the new sense of identity, but it will also provide the basis for organising new cultural industries through which we collectively develop and launch singers, musicians, film makers, writers, artists, poets, dancers and dramatists under a new multi-territory

'Caribbean' brand.

The new 'Caribbean' brand will also be the banner under which we construct new regional industries such as a modern Caribbean fishing industry equipped with a deep sea fishing fleet and a canning factory, a 'Caribbean' agro-processing industry through which we process the whole range of Caribbean agricultural products and market them to the world, and a new multi-territory, culturally advanced Tourism industry.

The Federation may also wish to look to the future by integrating Trinidad's petroleum industry with the solar energy and hydro electric initiatives of the other territories to create a comprehensive multi-faceted Caribbean energy industry.

Space does not permit us to outline details of all of the collectively planned initiatives that the youth, workers and entrepreneurs of the Union will have to take forward, but suffice it to say that such initiatives will also have to encompass the spheres of education, health, manufacturing, sport, food production, scientific research and development, national insurance and welfare systems, housing, seaport and highway development and water management and distribution.

Yes, it is time to write a new chapter in the history of the Caribbean. A brave new world beckons to us, and we must have the wisdom and courage to decide to be makers of history and to inaugurate the new era. And we can be sure that it will be an exciting and uplifting era in which we finally give our youth a mission that is capable of engaging their ambition, creative imagination and sense of self worth!

Chapter 19

I WANT TO RULE
MY DESTINY

IN concluding this submission on the establishment of a Federation or political union of the Caribbean, I will examine the relationship between the collective Federal government and the individual State governments, and propose a practical way forward on this issue.

Human nature being what it is, it is perhaps inevitable that there would be some tension between our new multi-territory Federal State and the individual states. This is to be expected. But the answer to this it to establish a core of strong directive political principles to guide us and keep such tension to manageable proportions.

For example, our brand of Caribbean federalism should mandate that as many decisions as possible are to be reached at the local member state level. We would therefore abjure the concept of 'centralism', with its mandate that everything be controlled and decided from one centre.

We would also need to have a clear understanding that the unity of the Federal State will be realised and preserved only if we respect the individuality of the various member states. Thus, member states must be permitted to enjoy a high degree of freedom in their political decisions, as well as a high degree of administrative autonomy.

DAVID COMISSIONG

Of course, each member state will continue to have its own individual constitution and laws. However, we would proceed on the basis that such constitutions and state laws will follow the broad outlines of the Federal constitution and legislation, but still allow for particular local needs.

Needless to say, the duties and powers of the Federal Government will be strictly defined and laid down in a new Federal Constitution. And generally speaking, the duty of the Federal Government will be to ensure internal and external security; to uphold and respect the constitutions and laws of the member states; to maintain diplomatic relations with foreign powers; and to undertake economic planning and development on a region-wide basis.

Some of the specific functions which will have to fall under the authority of the Federal Government are: customs, postal and telecommunication services, the monetary system, the military, civil law and regulations, criminal law, control of the common sea area, fisheries, air and sea transportation, region-wide economic planning, social security and the promulgation and upholding of human and civil rights.

Clearly, there will have to be a division of powers between the governments of the member states and the Federal Government, and a possible schema for such a division could be as follows:

(1) Those spheres in which the Federal Government is solely responsible for legislation. (These have been mentioned in some detail already).

(2) Those spheres that are exclusively the province of

the member states. Examples would include the police, social welfare, state provided housing, and religious affairs.

(3) Those spheres in which the Federal Government legislates and the state governments executes the legislation. Examples would include labour regulations, social security, the civil and criminal law, traffic regulations, military affairs and fisheries.

(4) Those spheres in which the power to legislate is shared between the Federal Government and the state governments. Examples would include taxation, education, road building, insurance and health services.

Perhaps the last mentioned category is the most intriguing category of them all—a category that is based on the creative sharing of rights and responsibilities between the Federal Government and the state governments. Let us examine this category in greater detail by looking at the example of education.

In the case of education, the most basic levels of the education system—the Primary and Secondary levels of schooling—could, for example, be the province of the member states, while the tertiary level, comprised of polytechnic and university education, could be controlled and regulated by the Federal Government. Of course, the CARICOM region already possesses the foundation of such a 'shared' approach to education, with our collectively operated regional university, the University of the West Indies.

It would be remiss of me to fail to mention that just as we already possess the basic structure of a Federal university system under the Treaty of Chaguaramas, we also already possess the following proto-Federal institutions: the Caribbean Court of Justice, Caribbean Disaster Emergency Response Agency, Caribbean Agricultural Research and Development Institute, Caribbean Food and Nutrition Institute, and the Caribbean Meteorological Organisation, among others.

And so, if there is already so much in place, what is holding us back? Is it a paucity of confidence; a lack of belief in ourselves and in our own people?

If this is the case, then it is now high time for us to put self-negating doubt behind us and stride forward to forge our collective destiny as a Caribbean people.

In the year 2011, the Clement Payne Movement, the Barbadian organisation that I have the privilege and honour of leading, drafted the text of a model Parliamentary resolution that laid down a 5-year timetable for the establishment of a Federation or political union of the Caribbean. We therefore end this dissertation by reproducing here the text of the said Resolution.

UNION OF CARIBBEAN STATES RESOLUTION

Acknowledging that the people of the 15 member states of the Caribbean Community (CARICOM) share a common geographical space, history and cultural identity, having undergone almost identical processes of European conquest and colonisation, forced migration from the continents of Africa, Asia and Europe, slavery, slave trade, indenture-ship, resistance to slavery and colonialism, emancipation, labour rebellion and organisation, de-colonisation and the conscious development of a Caribbean variety of political and cultural nationalism;

Cognizant that these common and shared realities have long impelled the people of these territories to conceive of the value and desirability of welding their relatively small separate states into one large unified multi-territory nation state under a Federal system of government;

Recalling that this popular conception of geographical, political, economic and cultural unity was embraced and nurtured by the early pioneers and architects of the Caribbean Labour Movement, and found its most forceful expression during the decades of the 1930s, 40s and 50s in the multiple demands of the 'Caribbean Labour Congress' for the de-colonisation and self-government of the British West Indian colonies under a unified, multi-territory Federal system of government;

Recognising that the progressive political wing of the Caribbean Labour Movement gave autonomous expression to these demands with the formation in 1956 of the West Indies Federal Labour party, a coalition of labour-oriented political parties based in the various British West Indian colonies;

Regretting that this deeply felt authentic popular desire for the establishment of a sovereign, independent, federated nation state of the Caribbean was frustrated and subverted through the British Colonial Office's imposition of a colonial, non-self-governing British West Indian Federation between the years 1958 to 1962;

Discerning that ever since the collapse of the British West Indies Federation in 1962 the people of the member states of the Caribbean Community (CARICOM) have been embarked on a collective journey back to realizing the unitary independent Federal nation state vision of the pioneers and architects of the Caribbean Labour Movement, a vision that is implicit in the work and ideals of the earliest craftsmen of Caribbean independence and nationhood – the leaders and statesmen of the Haitian Revolution;

Acknowledging that, to date, the most significant landmarks in this collective journey have been the establishment in 1968 of the Caribbean Free Trade Area (CARIFTA); its transformation in 1973 into the Caribbean Community and Common Market (CARICOM); the 1981 establishment of the Organisation of Eastern Caribbean States (OECS); the

1989 Grand Anse Declaration committing CARICOM to the creation of a Caribbean Single Market and Economy (CSME); the work and the 1992 report of the independent West Indian Commission; and the inauguration in 2006 of the Caribbean Single Market;

Conceding however, that while these institutions and measures of economic integration, intra-Caribbean trade facilitation, functional cooperation and coordination of external economic relations have been important achievements, yet they fall short of the ultimate goal of political union and collective nationhood, and do not provide the people of the Caribbean Community states with a strong enough mechanism for protecting their welfare and advancing their collective economic, cultural and political objectives;

Fully aware that the world has entered an era fraught with dangers and disadvantages for small developing nations, and characterised by a fundamental dislocation in the European and North American based international capitalist order and a relentless system of economic globalisation that is forcing small developing nations to expose themselves to the full blast of international competition;

Convinced that the only mechanism potent enough to protect the well being and welfare of the people of the Caribbean Community states, to create a concrete and practical basis for the development of a new regional industries and structures of production, to deliver enhanced economic and life opportunities to the masses of our people, to maintain the cultural uniqueness and integrity of our Caribbean region, and to ensure the continued existence of the sovereignty, independence and dignity of our people, is the merging of the separate nations of the Caribbean Community into one strong regional nation state.

It is now hereby resolved that the Government and people of Antigua, Bahamas, Belize, Barbados, Dominica, Guyana, Grenada, Haiti, Jamaica, St. Kitts & Nevis, St. Lucia, St. Vincent and the Grenadines, Suriname, Trinidad and Tobago:

1. **Agree** in principle with the idea of transforming the Caribbean Community (CARICOM) into a multi-territory politically unified, nation state existing under a Federal system of government.
2. **Commit** themselves to participating in a Constitutional Convention of the Caribbean Community (CARICOM) states to be held in one of the said CARICOM states commencing in the month of February in the year 2016, for the purpose of devising and agreeing upon the structure and Constitution of the said nation state, as well as the formula for ratifying the said Constitution and bringing the said nation state into existence;

3. **Commit** themselves to utilising the years and months between the adoption of this resolution and the month of February 2016 to engage in a comprehensive national consultation in their country that is designed to prepare their natural population for integration and participation in the new Federal nation state, and to discuss, devise and agree upon the ideas and proposals that the national delegates will put forward at the said Constitutional Convention;

4. **Agree** that the location and specific dates of the said Constitutional Convention shall be decided upon by a majority vote of the CARICOM heads of government assembled together in a CARICOM heads of government summit; and

5. **Agree** that each Caribbean Community (CARICOM) state that participates in the said Constitutional Convention shall be represented by a national delegation consisting of a maximum of 10 persons, of which number five shall be representatives of the governing political party, two shall be representatives of the political opposition represented in Parliament, and three shall be representatives of civil society.

We owe it to ourselves, our ancestors, and our posterity to take this step upwards on the ladder of sovereignty, self-determination and dignity. Our ancestors were brought to this Caribbean region in chains, and their oppressors separated them from each other, deposited them on a variety of small islands, and determined that they were to remain ever weak, divided and susceptible to exploitation. Let us ensure that we do not permit the evil agenda of our oppressors to become our lasting destiny. Let us instead— in the words of the Jamaican reggae singer—rule our destiny!

ROLL CALL
OF THE GIANTS OF THE CARIBBEAN
INTEGRATION MOVEMENT

Captain Arthur Cipriani
T.A. Marryshow
Marcus Mosiah Garvey
Sir Grantley Adams
Robert Bradshaw
Richard Hart
C.L.R. James
Dr. Eric Williams
Forbes Burnham
Elma Francois
W.A. Domingo
Richard B. Moore
Wynter Crawford
Sir Frank Worrell
Ebenezer Duncan
William Demas
Sir Arthur Lewis
Errol Barrow
Beryl McBurnie
Lloyd Best
Norman Manley

Michael Manley

Walter Rodney

Tim Hector

George Odlum

Maurice Bishop

Bob Marley

Rosie Douglas

Toussaint L'Ouverture

Jean Jacques Dessalines

Henry Christophe

Alexander Petion

DAVID COMISSIONG was born on the 17th April 1960 in the Caribbean island of St. Vincent. The son of a travelling Methodist Minister of Religion, David received his primary education at Tranquility Primary School in Trinidad, before attending Harrison College and the University of the West Indies (UWI) in Barbados.

He won a Barbados Exhibition in 1979 and the 'Sir Fred Phillips' academic prize at the Faculty of Law, University of the West Indies in 1981 and has been a practicing Attorney-at-law since 1984.

David Comissiong is a former Senator in the government of Barbados, and is currently the President of the opposition Peoples Empowerment Party (PEP).

He is also a founder-member and current President of the Clement Payne Movement of Barbados-one of the most important activist organizations of the Eastern Caribbean.

David has been a driving force in the Pan-African Movement over the past 20 years. He is a founder-member of the Pan-African Movement of Barbados (PAMOB), the Caribbean Pan-African Network (CPAN) and the Global

Afrikan Congress (GAC) and was an architect and the first Director of the Barbados Government's Commission For Pan-African Affairs (CPAA).

He represented the Caribbean region at the 7th Pan-African Congress in Uganda (1994), and played a key role in the United Nations' World Conference Against Racism in South Africa (2001).

Index

Post comments and questions about

this publication to:

www.facebook.com/widestreetsoftomorrow

www.ingramcontent.com/pod-product-compliance
Lightning Source LLC
Chambersburg PA
CBHW031207270326
41931CB00006B/444